Advanced Criminology or The WHY of Crimes

About the Author

Dr. James Vadackumchery, Criminologist & Advocate, M.A. (Crim.), D.Ph., LL.B., Ph.D., First rank holder for B.A. (Crim.) of Karnatak University and M.A. (Crim.) of Saugor University, Second rank holder for LL.B (Law) and D.Ph. examinations; Ph.D. in Criminal Justice (Kerala University), Gold Medalist and National Merit Scholarship Winner (twice).

Authentic author of more than 70 authoritative and research books in the special areas of Police, Crime and Justice and 1000 articles—research and popular—in professional journals, newspapers and periodical publications of repute.

Member of many professional organizations; Visiting Professor in universities and institutions of higher learning, research and training including Reserve Bank of India, National Judicial Academy etc.; Member, Board of Studies in Criminology of Karnatak, Calicut and Saugor Universities and State Advisory Board on Correctional Administration, Member, State Prison Review Committee (Kerala), Consultant to Police Welfare Commission, Public Speaker and Human Rights Activist, Broadcaster over AIR and Telecaster in Indian and International T.V. networks and a constant Consultant to the media (print and electronic) on criminological and human rights issues, Criminologist on the Faculty of the State Police Training College, Thiruvananthapuram for nearly three decades, now a practising lawyer.

A name in the International Dictionary of Biographies of the IBC, Cambridge, the recipient of the Distinguished International Scholar Award for Life Time Achievements—2003 of the American Society of Criminology, a name listed in the Limca Book of Records—2006 for authoring most books in crime, police and justice and a personality honoured by the University of Calcutta with Suprabha Deb Gold Medal—2007. Recipient of the Award of Excellence by the Archdiocese of Changanassery, 2007 and a PROFILE viewed by 5 per cent of 200 million people in Linked In during 2012.

Advanced Criminology
or
The WHY of Crimes

James Vadackumchery
Criminologist & Advocate

CONCEPT PUBLISHING COMPANY PVT. LTD.
NEW DELHI-110059

ISBN-13: 978-93-5125-265-8

First Published 2017

Published and Printed by

Concept Publishing Company Pvt. Ltd.
A/15-16, Commercial Block, Mohan Garden,
New Delhi-110059 (INDIA)
T : 25351460, 25351794
E : publishing@conceptpub.com, *W* : www.conceptpub.com

Cataloging in Publication Data--Courtesy: D.K. Agencies (P) Ltd. <docinfo@dkagencies.com>

Vadackumchery, James, author.
Advanced criminology or the WHY of crimes / James Vadackumchery.
pages cm
Includes bibliographical references and index.
ISBN 9789351252658

1. Criminology. 2. Criminology—Philosophy. 3. Criminal behavior. I. Title.

HV6025.V33 2017 DDC 364 23

Mary, Neethu, Neethie,
Anna, Maria, George, Ammu, Ann & Hannah

Preface

Once a devil was found bleeding and it was almost sinking. Then a Christian priest went through that way and found the devil in a very pathetic condition praying for help. The priest looked at it, and was about to leave the spot ignoring the ailing devil. The devil then called the priest and beckoned him. The devil asked him a charity and prayed : "Please take me to a hospital." The priest said in reply : "No, you are a devil and you instigate people to commit sins by temptations. I do not like you and you must die."

Hearing the priest, the devil smiled and said : "Look, you live and survive, because I work for you. If I do not work, then there will be no sinners and you will have no work if sinners are not there." The priest thought for a while and he took the sick devil to the best doctor available in the locality and got him treated.

The devils are said to be the most industrious spirits and they work day in and day out tempting people to commit sins/crimes. This is a famous story told by an eminent writer in his book which is one of the best sellers in the world.

Why do the people sin, i.e., violate the laws of God? In religion and up to eighteenth century, devil was accused to be the lone cause of sins/crimes. Demons instigate people by temptations and the innate depravity of man makes him to sin/commit crimes or violate the rules/laws etc. Criminology as a scientific discipline had its birth in the recent past and the study of the criminogenic factors began only with the positive school with Cessare Lombroso (1836-1909) who is eulogized as the father of modern criminology. He was an Italian physician, a prison doctor and a criminologist who said that atavism was the cause of crime. Atavism means the reappearance in an individual of characteristics of some remote ancestors that have been absent in intervening generations (Webster's). According to him, a criminal was an individual who embodied such a reversion i.e., atavism. He said that a criminal was a reversion to an earlier type, a throwback. Ever since, crime has been made a topic of research and scientific study. It was Topinard, a French Anthropologist who coined the word **criminology** by combining two words *Crimen* (Latin) which means crime and *Logos* (Greek) which means a study, discourse etc. Criminology is a scientific study of the etiology of crime and other related matters. Why do people commit crimes ? Thereafter, there came different disciplines taking special academic interest to study crimes and criminal behaviour. Philosophy, theology, anthropology, biology, sociology, statistics, genetics, psychology, psychiatry, endocrinology, victimology etc. have been just a few among the very many disciplines which take interest in the study of crime and criminal bahaviour.

There was a time people thought of individuals committing crimes and therefore, the studies were centred around individual and the causes of crimes and criminal behaviour. The penal codes were enacted on the basic assumption that crimes were committed only by individuals and therefore individuals were/are punished. Today crimes are found to be committed by groups and the society as a whole. In history, there was a time when a crime was considered as an offence committed against individuals. This approach of individuals *vs.* individuals was found to be injurious to social welfare and people's happiness. Many, especially the socially and economically handicapped people, did not/could not initiate any action/s against those who committed crimes against them. They had no option, but to suffer the ill-effects of crime and criminal behaviour. Thus, came the approach of treating crimes as offences committed against the society, people and the State.

Thus, the State became the investigator, prosecutor and the punishment giver. The questions which were then raised were—(i) Who committed the offence? (ii) Why was the offence committed ? (iii) How was the offence committed etc. In order to punish the criminal, the society/State wanted the "Why of Crimes." This book *Advanced Criminology or the WHY of Crimes* deals with the theory of crime causation.

I am the first Government appointed criminologist in the State of Kerala (1976) and I was working with the police department—studying, teaching, researching many aspects of crime and criminal behaviour. This book contains my research observations about the causation of crime and the theory is called the *push-pull-ego factor* approach. The study was conducted in India and U.S.A. and the findings exposed in my earlier book *Contemporary Indian Criminology* are further elaborated in this book *Advanced Criminology or the WHY of Crimes*. A survey of literature about the etiology of crime gives me enough evidence to assert that the *ego factor* which is formed by an interaction between the *push* and *pull factors* (in the ego or personality) is an important force or energy to commit crimes. According to my researches, the *push factors* which consist of *animality, spirituality, morality/ethics and intelligence* have a say in the commission of crimes/in desisting from the commission of crimes. The *pull factors* which are nothing but the surrounding environments have interactions with the *push factors* and with the help of these *push* and *pull factors* and the *ego factor,* the causation of crimes is explained in this book.

Throughout the text, one may read *ego, ego factor, push factors, pull factors* etc., and I like to clarify the meaning of each one of them. *Ego* in Webster's means, "The 'I' or 'Self' of any person; a person as thinking, feeling and willing, and distinguishing itself from the selves of others and from objects of its thought." In psycho-analysis, *Ego* means the part of the psychic apparatus that experiences and reacts to the outside world and thus mediates between the primitive drives of the id and the demands of the social and physical environment. In philosophy, it means the enduring and conscious element that knows experience. In scholasticism, it is the complete person comprising both body and soul. In ethnology, it means a person who serves as the central reference point in the study of organizational and kinship relationship (Webster's). These aspects are again brought or repeated in the text as well to make matters clear. In the *push-pull-ego factor* theory/approach, the *Ego Factor* is used as an activating force or energy to behave as an individual or personality. Personality in Psychology, according to Webster's, is the sum total of the physical, mental, emotional, and social characteristics of an individual; organized pattern of behavioural characteristics of the individual.

Whenever I use the word **Ego,** i.e., (i) **Spirituality Ego,** I mean the **energy** or **force** which pushes an individual to activate himslef in a given situation. In **Spirituality Ego,** the activating energy or force is the **faith or belief or both;** (ii) **Morality/Ethics Ego** means the activating force or energy to interact with the **pull factors** (situations) with or without any **guilt feelings;** (iii) **Intelligence Ego** is the activating energy to interact with the **Pull Factors** or situations with memory, comprehension, expansion, critical analysis or/and intuitiveness/inventiveness; and (iv) **Animality Ego** is nothing but the activating force or energy to interact with the **Pull Factors** in an instinctive way or instinctively. Accordingly, **Ego Factor** means the activating force or energy which an individual (personality) has as a unique person and it is formed as the effect of the interactions between **push** and **pull factors.**

Push Factors in a man are the **animality + inteligence + morality/ethics** and **spirituality egos** as they move a person/individual in a specified way by exerting force. **Pull factors** around a person/individual are the situations which draw him/her in a particular direction or into a particular position. The situations may be social, economic, educational, religious, financial, health, moral, racial, regional, political and thus there may be many which pull a person with or without his/her knowledge or awareness. The **push** and **pull factors** interact and ultimately an **ego factor** is formed and it is this **ego factor** which interacts with **pull factors** which come in one's life. Depending upon the dominating **ego factor** in a given situation, a person/individual commits crimes. If and when **animality** is expressed without any control or reservations by **morality/ ethics, spirituality** and **intelligence,** it is likely that a crime is committed depending upon the laws of the land. Again the same thing takes place whenever other **ego factors** namely **morality/ethics, spirituality** or **intelligence** act as the activating force. Anything beyond a limit may be a crime. All these aspects are discussed in detail in the chapters that follow.

The first chapter of this book i.e., **Criminology Down the Millenia** brings out the etiological explanations and findings from Demonology to Victimology. It treats the etiology from **causality** as well as from **causation** angles. Chapter **2** is about **Individual, Groups and Society.** Today crimes are committed by individuals, groups and the society as a whole. The approach of finding out the etiology from a purely individualistic angle is no more valid and acceptable today. Hence, the etiology of crime from the angle of group and society need to be analyzed and studied. In Chapter 3, the **Animality** as a powerful factor to activate man's behaviour is discussed. The root cause of every crime and criminal behaviour is found to be an animal instinct or more of them. In Chapter 4, the **Intelligence** as a powerful factor to distinguish/differentiate human behaviour from animal behaviour is brought out. Chapter 5 is all about **Morality**—a factor to control human behaviour. It contains everything from divine law to folklore assumptions/rules to control man and his behaviour. Chapter 6 brings out **Spirituality**—a factor to propel people forward in behaviour by resolving his frustrations/conflicts etc. with a hope to go ahead with faith in God/gods or belief in a Cosmic Power/Universal Force/Absolute-Eternal Principle or with both—i.e., an invisible spirit. Chapter 7 is all about **Push factors and pull factors**. Chapter 8 is my **Theory in criminology.**

Earlier, I wrote a book titled, **Contemporary Indian Criminology** when I spent some time in Bentonville, Arkansas, U.S.A., with my sweet daughter, Neethie and my little grand daughter, Maria during 2010-11 and got it published by Concept Publishing Company (Pvt.) Ltd., New Delhi. It contained an exposure of this theory which I got published in research journals still earlier. There have been demands from many parts of the world—*via* **LinkedIn** and otherwise—for further expansion of my theory on crime causation. That is a reason why I bring out this title: **Advanced Criminology or the WHY of Crimes** now. Again, Neethie provided me all facilities to write this book at Euless, Dallas Fort Worth, U.S.A. and I thank my daughter Neethie, grand daughters Maria, Ann and my wife for their liberal support to bring out this book. Now, we have Hannah, a baby girl born in Neethie's family and thus I am grateful to all of them and Concept Publishing Company (Pvt.) Ltd., New Delhi for their wholehearted encouragement to bring out this book in print.

January 7, 2016
Euless, Dallas Fort Worth
U.S.A.

James Vadackumchery
Criminologist & Advocate

Contents

Contents

List of Figures

Eureka

Eureka—I have found it

This is the reputed exclamation of Archimedes (287 ?-212 B.C.) when, after long study, he discovered a method of detecting the amount of alloy mixed with the gold in the crown of the King of Syracuse. My 40-45 years of study in criminology gives me enough confidence to give a theory of crime causation. Crime is an act or omission (action or an instance of negligence) that is considered injurious to public welfare or morals or religious divine teachings or to the interests of the State, and that is legally prohibited. Thus, I find antisocial acts, immoral acts/vices, sins, offences and wrongs as crimes. They are seen from the birth of man in this universe. I do not claim that the **push-pull ego factor** theory of crime causation is a mammoth *Eureka* in criminology, nevertheless I proudly feel that my theory is a humble *Eureka* to understand the etiology of crimes and criminal behaviour, no matter, they are traditional, modern, contemporary, current or individual, group, society or moral, ethical, religious, cultural, institutional or national, international, corporate or juvenile, women, old age or racial, caste, subcaste, communal, regional, linguistic or human rights, humanitarian, victimological etc. **Push-pull-ego factor** theory is not theory of causality, but it is a theory of crime causation.

A search for the **why** of crimes has a long history from demology to victimology for administering a total and holistic justice. Here, the theory is simple, i.e.,

(1) Man is born with a heredity which interacts with the environment and forms the personality or ego.

(2) Man has four activating forces-**EGOS-**in his mind known as **animallity, spirituality, morality/ethics** and **intelligence.** They are mixed together in such a way that the human mind works as one-the four energies in the **ego** are put under **push factors.**

(3) There are very many-*innumerable numbers-seen and unseen-heard and unheard-known and unknown-* environmental forces and situational factors around a man and all of them are put together to call them PULL FACTORS.

(4) From the birth of a child, the **PUSH** and **PULL FACTORS** interact to form an **EGO** and **EGO FACTOR.** It is seen that the **foundation** of the **EGO** and **EGO FACTOR** is laid down by the time a person reaches his puberty. As a man grows older and older, the super structure is constructed on this **foundation** and thus the **EGO FACTOR** gets modified to that extent. Like an individual, a group and a society as a whole will have an **EGO FACTOR** formed in due course.

(5) Whenever a man-a group-a society-is exposed to situations in life, the **PUSH FACTORS (animality + morality/ethics + intelligence + spirituality)** either fight or cooperate with the situations which are the **PULL FACTORS** at the given time i.e.,

$$\textbf{C.B.} = \left\{ \begin{array}{c} \textbf{PULL FACTORS} \text{ divided by } \textbf{PUSH FACTORS} \\ \text{or} \\ \textbf{PULL FACTORS} \text{ multiplied by } \textbf{PUSH FACTORS} \end{array} \right\}$$

In other words—

$$\frac{\textbf{PULL FACTORS}}{\textbf{PUSH FACTORS}} \div$$

or **PULL FACTORS × PUSH FACTORS**

Where

C.B. is Criminal Behaviour

The theory says—

1. When interaction takes place between the **PUSH FACTORS** in the already formed **EGO** or **PERSONALITY** and the **PULL FACTORS** presently available, a crime is committed if and when the **PULL FORCES** overpower the **PUSH FORCES.** In other words, an atmosphere contaminated with criminality or saturated with crimes exists, then commission of crime is the only option as the **EGO FACTOR** in the **PERSONALITY** is weak and incapable to fight with the **PULL FORCES.**
2. When the interaction takes place between **PUSH FACTORS** in the already formed **EGO or PERSONALITY** and **PULL FACTORS,** a crime is committed if and when the **ANIMALITY** with out the support of other **PUSH FORCES** overpowers the **PULL FORCES,** putting down the effects of other **PUSH FACTORS** like **MORALITY/ETHICS, SPIRITUALITY and INTELLIGENCE.**
3. When the interaction takes place between the **PUSH FORCES** in the already formed **EGO or PERSONALITY** and **PULL FACTORS,** a crime is committed in a well calculated and planned way if and when the **ANIMALITY** and **INTELLIGENCE** jointly work and overpower the **PULL FORCES** lessening down the effects of other **PUSH FACTORS** like **MORALITY/ETHICS** and **SPIRITUALITY.**
4. A crime is some times committed by **ANIMALITY** with the support of either **SPIRITUALITY** or **MORALITY/ETHICS** (and in some cases both) as the case may be.
5. Whenever the criminal prone **PUSH FACTORS** interact with **PULL FACTORS** which are crime prone by cooperation, then crimes will be the inevitable net result of such interactions.

6. The same theory is applicable in the case of individuals, groups or society alike.

Crimes can only be controlled or reduced in number. They can never be prevented in toto or eliminated from the society. If a particular type of crime is reduced, then there will come up another type of a similar crime. Thus crimes are altered and never destroyed just like the energy which is neither created nor destroyed. It is changed from one form to another. Crimes are constant in a given society and I advocate a **QUOTA THEORY** of crime and I adhere to such an approach. Hence, reduction of crimes is possible and never their erradication at any stage/level. Man is blessed or condemned to live in crimes and amidst criminals. For, every human act/omission is an act/omission prohibitted by some law or another; permitted by some law or another.

Introduction

Why human beings behave the way they do?—This was my first lecture at the Police Training College, Thiruvananthapuram when I joined on the Teaching Faculty there in 1976. Police officers who attended an in-service course said: ***"because of their motives"***. O.K., I admitted. They assumed that human behaviour was motivated. Then one ought to know: ***"What is motivation?"*** It is *"an inner influence on behaviour as represented by physiological condition, interests, attitudes and aspirations."* In common parlance, people do not make my distinctions among motivations, intentions, motives, drives, needs, instincts etc. They use them as one and the same although they have special and specific meanings. In psychology, motives are, as a rule, classified into three groups, namely—

(i) Those which are closely tied up or connected or associated with the physical needs like hunger (survival needs).

(ii) Those which are not tied up or connected to or associated with the physiological processes like sex (expansion *via* reproduction needs).

(iii) Those which are acquired or learned like need for recognition.

Out of them, physical or physiological needs (like need for oxygen, water, food etc.) make the human organism to seek for them. They are positive motives. Like the positive motives, there will be negative motives too. Avoidance of physical pains, extreme coldness, foul smell, unpalatable tastes etc. is noticed as they cause discomfort, irritation, threat, displeasure etc. Unlike the above motives, which are closely connected, there are a few like sex, maternal instincts etc. which are not closely tied up with the physiological needs. There are '*Brahmacharis*' who piously avoid sex and in certain religious sects people take '*chastity*' as their religious vow and they keep it up as sacred till death. They too eat moderately and drink as they connot survive without them. The chaste priests, *pujaris,* nuns, *sannyasis, sadhus* and so on take it as their holy vow. People become religious and the Christians, Catholics, Protestants, Evangelists, Anglicans, Hindus, *Brahmins, Kshatriyas, Vaishyas, Shudras, Dalits, Adivasis,* Muslims, Shias, Sunnies, Sikhs, Jains, Parsis, Jews and so on develop their motives through learning and the learned motives may be specific or general. Psychologists say that the development of positive or negative attraction is a learned response. It is empirically proved that positive, negative or neutral feelings are found to be strong motives affecting one's behaviour.

The participants to the above in-service course continued to give more reasons to *"why human beings behave the way they do?"* According to them, it could be owing to:

(i) Instincts, i.e., "an organized and relatively complex mode of response, characteristic of a given species, that has been phylogenetically adapted to a specific type of environmental situation" (Warren, H.C., *Dictionary of Psychology,* 1934).

"An innate or inherited psychophysical disposition which (determines) makes the organism to attend to certain kind of objects rather than others, to experience an emotional excitement of a particular quality upon perceiving such an object and to act in regard to it in a particular manner or atleast to experience an impulse to such an action" (McDougall).

In my book, **Contemporary Indian Criminology,** published by Concept Publishing Co. (P) Ltd., New Delhi, 2015, I have extensively dealt with **instincts** when I discussed the **Push-Factors** in crime causation. I admitted the fact that instincts play an important role in human behaviour although psychologists have different views about instincts, drives, motives, motivational dynamics etc. Instincts (drives in man) in my view are the **Push Factors** in the commission of crimes.

(ii) Emotions, i.e., a complex feeling state accompanied by characteristic motor and glandular activities. (English, H.B. and English, A.C., *A Comprehensive Dictionary of Psychological and Psychoanalytical Terms*, Logmans, Green, New York, 1958).

I did not or better, could not agree with them as I was of the view that emotions were just expressions which followed instincts. Whenever man becomes emotional, he gets unexpected strength and surcharged energy. Precisely therefore, the common man says: "When passion comes, reason flies away." Most of the people are able to identify several categories of emotions although some may fail to recognize a particular emotion as it is. Expressions of emotion are universal although some psychologists do not subscribe to this view. Anyway, the participants needed more information about emotions to speak about their importance in behavioural dynamics. Emotions will show how one exhibits/expresses/exposes his instincts (drives) and will never become a **Push Factor** in the commission of crimes.

(iii) Complexes, i.e., "a group of repressed ideas interlinked into a complex whole which besets the individual, impelling him to think, feel and perhaps act after a habitual pattern." (R.J. Campbel, *Psychiatric Dictionary,* Oxford University Press, New York, 1981).

Oedipus Complex, Electra Complex, Diana Complex, Demosthenes Complex, Clytemnestra Complex, Clerambault-Kandinsky Complex, Cain Complex, Inferiority Complex etc. are some of them. I have no difficulty to accept their views, but I wanted to tell them that the root causes of the complexes were very important. Complexes did influence people to behave in a particular way, but were not the only causes behind the behaviour of people. Hence, one must look behind and beyond complexes, when he makes a search to identify the etiology of human behaviour.

(iv) Unconscious, i.e., the concept of ***unconscious*** is seen in Freudian Psychoanalytic school for treating people suffering from psychic disorders and precisely therefore, I was not very much interested to have an elaborate discussion on ***unconscious*** and human behaviour. We are concerned about: "why the normal human beings behave the way they do" and not at all on patients who need psychoanalytic treatment. Of course, I have no difficulty to accept that all people have motives, feelings, memories and thoughts of which they are absolutely unaware of. Certainly, I admit that the unconscious motives do affect human behaviour in a significant way, but are not the only causes behind one's behaviour.

(v) Personality, i.e., the personality traits which are nothing, but the enduring pattern of behaviour. There are one thousand and one traits—positive, negative or neutral. I have research evidence to show that personality traits are not the causes of human behaviour, rather will, decide how one may behave if he commits a criminal act. For example, cruelty is a personality trait and it does not mean that all people who exhibit cruelty will become criminals. At the same time, if he/she commits a crime (e.g., murder), it will be cruelly executed. Precisely therefore, personality and personality traits in an individual cannot become a **Push Factor** in the commission of crimes.

(vi) Learning, i.e., people learn to commit crime. Differential Association theory of Prof. Edwin H. Sutherland subscribes to this view and my researches give me ample evidence to show that learning does not make a person to commit crimes. And differential association approach is unacceptable to me precisely because an association with others does not/cannot push a person to commit crimes. It may teach one the mechanics of committing crimes in a professional way and some times with expertise. Many who spend their sentence in prisons with inmates do not become recidivists although some may. The differential association therefore cannot be a **Push Factor** in the commission of crimes. However, the differential association and facilities to have differential association may be a **Pull Factor.** The opportunity received for learning also can be considered as a **Pull Factor.** Certainly, the

Push Factor along with **Pull Factor** may result in an **Ego Formation** and to that extent, Sutherland's theory of differential association is acceptable to explain the sociological causation of crimes. Socialization and formation of conscience in an upright way in the right direction will be of interest while examining the causation of crimes.

(vii) Constitution, i.e., the biological make up of the indiviual including both innate and acquired assets and liabilities. Physique, sex, temperament, endocrine functioning and body types are some of the characteristics included in this category [James C. Coleman, *Abnormal Psychology and Modern Life,* D.B. Tarapowala Sons & Co. (Pvt.) Ltd., Bombay, 1964].

Kretschmer's classification or Sheldon's classification spoke a lot about body types and causation of crimes. Their approaches were rejected by later researchers in criminology. I am of the view that Constitution can never become a **Push Factor** or **Pull Factor** in the formation of **Ego.** They have nothing much to do with animal behaviours and so is the case with human behaviour including criminal behaviour.

(viii) Physiology, i.e., the sense organs, effectors, endocrime glands, respiratory and nervous systems—it is found—do decide the dynamics of behaviour including criminal behaviour. Sense may deceive man and Shri Sankara spoke about **Maya**—the rope appearing to be a snake in the twilight. This is a classical example. The artificial lights may affect the vision and there may take deception of the colour. There may be auditory deceptions etc. Admitting the inability of the senses to perceive things in the way they are, I am of the view that the senses do not and cannot activate a man to behave in a particular way. A man may helplessly behave in a partucular way and it does not mean that the senses activate him to behave in that way. There may be illusions and miscalculations about the height, width, depth etc. and a man may take an indifferent attitude to issues, events and individuals even when his senses perceive things in a particular way.

There was a time when endocrinologists argued that a man commits crimes owing to endocrine malfunctionings. Researches could establish that the findings were far away from being real. Endocrines do not activate a man to behave in a particular way. My own researches prove that the endocrine glands and their secretions including malfunctioning can regulate or influence bodily activities, but can never activate a man to behave in a particular way or in a criminal way.

What about the biological energy level, autonomic reactivity resistence to stress and the quality and the stability of the central nervous system in activating people to behave in a special or specific way and particularly in criminal way? There is evidence to show that the energy and activity level of a person are apparently related to whether or not he develops aggressive or more internalized reactions to stress. Autonomic reactivity—high emotional reactivity—is found to be related to overreaction to minor stresses and deficient emotional reactivity is seen to be related to inadequate socialization. Emotions accompany instincts and precisely therefore the autonomic reactivity—i.e., high emotional reactivity—is connected or associated with instincts.

(ix) Chromosomal abnormality, i.e., there exist numerous chromosomal abnormalities and scientists attribute antisocial behaviours (For example, alcoholism and homosexuality) to XXY or Klinefelter syndrome. However, this finding was rejected by later researches and asserted that the causative factors behind criminal behaviour should be located elsewhere, other than chromosomes and their abnormalities.

(x) Congenitaly acquired defects, i.e., physically handicapped people (socially handicapped, economically handicapped, religiously, communally, racially handicapped as well)—whether the deformities are congenital or acquired suffer from difficulties in adjustment. They are seen to have—(1) feeling of inferiority, (2) self-pity, (3) hostility, (4) stubbornness, (5) arrogance, (6) obstinacy, (7) undue anxiety, and (8) rage. Why? Squint or cat's eye, shortness, pitch black colour, lone or protruded teeth, lameness, albenism, body fatness (bulky) or obesity etc. create adjustment problems. Why? **Push-Pull-Ego Factor** Theory of Crime Causation has an answer to such problems and behaviour.

(xi) Defective psychological development, i.e., inadequate/defective development of psyche or the "psychodynamic factors" within the individual create problems. Everyone has the potency for the development of desirable personality traits and the **Pull Factors** (i.e., the environment) provide opportunities for their proper or improper developments. The **Ego** formed as a result of the interaction between the hereditary potencies **(Push Factors)** and the environment **(Pull Factors)** make the foundation for the **EGO** in a neonate. Inadequate maternal care, improper mothering and parenting, distorted mother-infant (parent-child) relationship, difficulties in feeding etc. are seen to be causally connected to undesirable behaviour in a developing child in its environmental evaluations, habits of thinking and patterns of behaviour in later life. Rejection, indifferent or punishing mother (parents), quarrelsome family, neglect at home etc. cause unthinkable havoc in the personality formation of a developing child. The children in such situations may show negativistic behaviour. Lack of love, too much of love, harsh treatment, unhappy family, broken home, too-lax father, authoritarian or permissive parent, lack of family solidarity, parental inconsistency, parental discrimination for a favourite child etc. are found resulting in rebellion, quarrelsome habits, personality problems etc. which may lead to delinquent behaviour. (*Human Behaviour and Law Enforcement, Criminology and Penology* by James Vadackumchery). More about the ***Ego*** formation will be treated elaborately in the chapters that follow.

(xii) Mental conflicts and frustrations in life, i.e., anything which disturbs the mental equilibrium will make a person to have recourse to various defence mechanisms or escape mechanisms. The mechanisms may be (i) invert or (ii) overt. If one resorts to overt mechanisms, he may express/exhibit criminal behaviour. Why? **Push-Pull-Ego Factor** Theory of crime causation has an answer to the question.

At the very outset, it may be clarified that crime is a human behaviour and very much a social reality. A man is not a criminal, but there is a "criminal" in everyman. The question here is: "can a man be a criminal always?—everywhere?—every time?" No, he cannot and he is not, if at all he wants to be. A man is called "a man"—for, primarily he is a man and then only he becomes a crime-doer or a criminal or a convict. Every human act has criminal contents and people fail to or refuse to take note of such contents.

- Criminal is a man who exists and non-criminal is a concept and he does not exist. In other words, crime is a reality whereas no crime is a myth.
- The fact that man commits crime shows that only man will and can commit crimes. There exists no crimes among animals, birds, reptiles, fishes and insects.
- Behind every crime there is a criminal and there are conditions inducing criminality in people. The conditions inducing criminality are as important as or more important than the criminal himself.
- After all, crimes are acts or omissions which violate the laws—sociological, spiritual, religious, institutional or any of such... *cals.*
- What is a crime after all? It is an act or omission which some people dare to do at times. Criminals, in that sense, are courageous ones!
- Crime is a process and it will go on in different ways so long as man lives on this earth.
- Crime-doers or criminals are as much a part of the society as teachers, policeman, businessmen and professionals. Every criminal is a product of the society in which he lives and every society gives him the methods, ideals and goals.
- Punishment to crime-doers is as old as crime itself and the crime is as old as the humanity.
- No one is born as a man/woman. Everyone is changed into a man/woman. And this is true in the case of criminals too.

With those thoughts in mind, the **Push-Pull-Ego Factor** Theory must be appreciated. For, it explains why do human beings commit crimes?—Why does a group commit crimes?—Why does a society commit crimes?

INDIVIDUAL, GROUP AND SOCIETY

Push-Pull-Ego Factor theory accepts the research evidence that the forces which affect the individual and the forces which affect the group and the society at large to commit the crimes are one and the same. There exists no difference in the forces. For example: (1) When an individual commits a property offence, the activating instinctual force is **acquisitiveness.** This is true in the case of a group or a society when they involve in the commission of property offences.

(2) When a group commits an offence against human body (e.g., attacking a person/another group) the instinctual force will be **Pugnacity** (combat) and the same is true in the case of individuals as well as society committing the same offence.

Crimes are nothing but the violation of law. The law may be social, cultural, moral, ethical, religious or penal (State-made) and the forces behind all sorts of crime and criminal behaviour will be the instincts. For, instincts alone can or will activate animals and humans. Of course, man does have something more than what the animals have for activation. The instinctual forces are put under **Animality.** Man cannot behave just like the animals behave. For, he is controlled by **Morality/Ethics, Spirituality, Intelligence.** How do they interact to form the **push factors** is discussed in detail in the chapters that follow. My researches do not prove that there exist criminal motivations as William Bonger said long ago. There is nothing called criminal motivations. What one sees in existence are the animal instincts—nothing more and nothing less. Animal instincts which are necessary for **activation** cannot become criminal. If they act beyond the borderline, they may not be good for harmonious life in society or social welfare. In such situations, people call the animal instincts to be criminal instincts or criminal motivations and I have my reasoned objections to accept them otherwise. Why? It is like saying: *"The sun does not rise in the **east** in the morning. The spot where the sun is seen in the morning is called **east** by us."*

It is accepted that man is an evolution from animal and precisely therefore he has/should have animality in him.

Animality means '**instincts**' and they are for activating animals to behave. These instincts are not controlled in animals. Hence, they behave as they want. In man, the differentiating element is his intelligence which the early philosophers/scientists named as **rationality.** Behavioural scientists during the early part of the twentieth century proved that intelligence is not **rationality** alone, rather it contains many more—namely **intuitiveness, inventiveness, memory, comprehension, expansion** etc. Hence, they said that man is an **Intelligent Animal.**

An intelligent animal cannot and should not behave the way it wants. He has to co-exist with others and therefore scientists found out another content (just like intelligence) in man, i.e., **Morality/Ethics.** This content controls, regulates and pressures people to behave in a particular way for human co-existence and harmonious living. All laws, rules, regulations, customs, traditions which are there to control man's behaviour may be seen in **Morality/Ethics** sphere of human mind. Hence, they said that man is a **Moral/Ethical** animal.

As an **intelligent** and **moral/ethical** animal, the man behaves. But, there will be road-blocks and he finds it difficult to go further hopefully. He needs an assurance that moves him hopefully forward. Scientists found it to be an **invisible** or **spiritual force/power.** Hence, man moves forward with some **Beliefs** or/and **Faith.** Those who have **faith** in an invisible power called that **spirit** to be **God/gods.** People find extreme pleasure and mental satisfaction whenever they pleased that **Absolute Eternal Cosmic Power** called **God/gods.** Some made that **power** to be their personal God and thus many religions came into existence. People who did not have a religion/ religious God/gods made their own God/gods for worship. Those who do not have **faith** in an invisible God/gods need **belief** in some Cosmic Power/Eternal or Absolute Principles for their onward journey. Most of the people have both **faith** and **belief** and a few have only **belief** (not **faith**). Hence, scientists put **spirituality** too and called man to be an **intelligent, moral/ethical, spiritual animal.** This book brings out all those truths put in a theory called **push-pull-ego factor** theory and the theory is made use of to explain criminal behaviour. It may be clarified at the outset that the theory is not a theory of **causality,** rather is a theory of **crime causation.**

1
Criminology: Down the Millenia

Three men—a medical doctor, an engineer and a politician—were making an argument about "whose profession started first in human history?"

Medical Doctor: "God created Eve after conducting a surgery on Adam and He created Eve from the rib of Adam—this is seen in the Holy Bible."

Engineer: "Ha, ha, ha! God created man on the last day and the surgery was done only when Eve was created. The Bible says that God created everything prior to his creation of man." God said: "let there be light" and thus everything was created. His argument was that creation itself is an engineer's task and therefore his profession started first in human history.

Politician laughed at their argument and said: "In the Bible it is written that God created everything out of **chaos** and he asked further: **'who created the chaos?'** and according to him, politician's job started first in human history."

Forget about their arguments. When God created people, he created man and woman—thus is seen in the Holy Bible. God provided to them everything in the paradise and gave them this command. The command was: *"You may eat indeed all of all the trees in the garden. Nevertheless of the tree of the knowledge of good and evil you are not to eat, for on the day you eat of it you shall most surely die."*

What did Adam and Eve do? The first thing they did after their creation was to violate the command of God. Hence, crime is as old as humanity. For, crime is the violation of a law (command), no matter, it is God-given or man-made. Sins, vices, immoral acts, evil doings, crimes, offences, anti-social acts, asocial behaviour are related and hail from the same family. They show the law violating behaviour of man and the laws may be, as said earlier, religious, ethical, moral, social, cultural, institutional, State-made, caste-made, personal, regional, local, international and what not? Everyone violates some laws and thus everyone is a criminal in some same way or other. Hence, the question: "Why does a man commit a crime?" In my book **"Crime, Police and Correction"** published by A.P.H. Publishing Corporation, New Delhi, 1998, I wrote:

1. *There are multiplicity of factors which influence a person to behave in a particular way. If one's behaviour is criminal in nature and content, it means that there are several causative factors to make him do the way he does. Try to have an insight into the etiological factors.*
2. *A criminal is born-no-he is made. There is a third view, i.e., heredity and environment work together to make a person to commit a crime.*
3. *Crimes are committed by little children, adults and the old. The forces—or the causative factors—which work in all of them are different only in degrees and not in kind.*

I have actively worked with the police over 30 years and have closely observed the causative aspects of crime and criminal behaviour. Precisely, therefore, I want to make a distinction between a theory of **causality** and a theory of **crime-causation.**

THEORY OF CAUSALITY AND THEORY OF CAUSATION OF CRIME AND CRIMINAL BEHAVIOUR

I studied Philosophy and Theology for some time in my life and there we studied about the theory of causality. Basically, the theory says that *"There is no effect without a cause"* and alternatively *"There is no cause without an effect"*. Theology tells us that "God is the **cause** of everything." This approach—i.e., the cause, effect or effect, cause explanation is what is taught in the *theory of causality.*

Examples are plenty and the often quoted ones are—

1. No child without a father. Here, the father and child have cause-effect relationship.
2. No smoke without fire—Here, the fire and smoke have cause-effect relationship.

Counter arguments are there for the theory of causality. For, father alone cannot become the cause of a child. There should be a mother, i.e., spermatozoon[1] and ovum. There must be a conducive atmosphere/environment for conception and development. Again, fire alone cannot cause smoke. There should be a facilitating environment (Oxygen) for the fire to cause smoke. Still, the fact remains that there cannot be or will not be the **effect** without them. In other words, there will not be a **child** without a **father.** There will not be **smoke** without **fire.** Father is the *conditio sine-qua non* for the child and fire is the condition without which there will not be any smoke. The relationship between the cause and effect is such that one cannot exist without the other. In criminology or in a study of the causative aspects of crime, the **theory of causality** has no relevance or applicability as one cannot say specifically or with certainty that a particular crime has "such and such cause or causes." There is no cause-effect relationship between a crime (effect) and its often stated causes in criminology.

What is studied in criminology? It is nothing but the etiological or causative factors behind a crime. In demonology, the **devil** was said to be the cause of crime. In other words, devil's instigation and the innate deprivity of man were considered to be the causes of crime. No crime without the devil and it means that there existed a cause-effect relationship between the devil (as the **cause**) and the crime (as the **effect**). Wherever crime existed, the devil was a must. Devil[2] means an evil spirit and precisely therefore one had to banish the devil if he wanted to escape from the commission of crime. Hence, exorcism and occult practices to banish the devil (evil spirit) were the only option for the people to escape from the commission of crimes. I found: "All men commit crimes. Nevertheless, the attitude to commit crimes, the frequency in committing crimes and the persistence in continuing with the commission of crimes are more important than the actual commission of crimes." According to the theory of causality, it is possible to get out of the commission of crimes if and only if the evil spirits are thrown out from their influences. For it, people had recourse to exorcism and even today, there are people who firmly believe the influence of the evil spirits in man. This belief is seen in very many people from *Adivasis* to people advanced in knowledge and academic pursuits, in administrators, political leaders, religious men, moralists, theologians and so on. Devils have got scope even today as the single **cause** of crime and many people survive and make a living on such a belief. They make money and make a life-luxurious life, some times, in a very prosperous way. Spiritualists, devil banishers, evil spirit killers, occult practitioners, devil worshippers and preachers, *durmantravadis* (people who perform black magic for expelling evil spirits), soothsayers and so on prosper in society because of this theory of causality.

What were the **single cause** explanations of crimes in history? Besides and apart from devils, they were—

1. Freedom of will, hedonism and crime. 2. Criminal motivations and facilitating environments. 3. Exploitation of workers. 4. Lack of education. 5. Inadequate recreational facilities. 6. Defective glandular functioning. 7. Police corruption. 8. Neglect in religious teachings. 9. Emotional instability. 10. Lack of intelligence.

11. Frustration of the fundemental satisfaction drives. 12. Mental conflicts. 13. Broken homes, disorganized families. 14. Divorced, deserted or separated families. 15. Unemployed or underemployed families. 16. Inadequate formaion of super-ego. 17. Overeffect of "Id" complexes. 18. 'Unconscious' in man. 19. 'Subconscious' in people.

20. Poverty, unemployement, underemployment. 21. Affluence in money and luxuries. 22. Atavism and born-criminal approach. 23. Emotionally unstable nature. 24. No fear of punishments. 25. No proper law enforcement. 26. Administration of wounded justice. 27. Defective law and order management. 28. *'isms'* and *'ologies'* in politics. 29. Geography and topography. 30. Alcoholism and drug addiction.

31. Climate, thermal theory, hot climate, cold climate. 32. Authority, authoritarian attitude and approaches. 33. Miscarriage of justice, bribery and corruption, partiality and partisan attitude in justice administration. 34. Lack of justness in police work, lack of punishment, unfairness in police approaches. 35. Desire to commit crimes, delusion to commit crimes, obstinate determination to commit crimes. 36. No option, but to commit crimes. 37. Inefficiency of police and crime detecting agencies. 38. Failure in investigation. 39. Expression of maladjusted personality, personality disorders.

40. Mental defectiveness, emotional disturbance. 41. Lack of cultural and moral education. 42. Unfavourable circumstances and crime producing environments. 43. No character and proper conscience formation. 44. Ignorance of law, opportunities to commit crimes. 45. Courage in committing crimes. 46. Sex, women and liquor. 47. Victim participation. 48. Victim precipitation. 49. Victim incitement, provoking, inviting, conniving, prompting. 50. Victim-victimizer relationship.

51. Age, immaturity in understanding. 52. Legal immunity. 53. Mania, moral insanity. 54. Unawareness of the nature of crime. 55. Phobia. 56. Social inheritance and sociopathy. 57. Psychological inheritance and psychopathy. 58. Personality traits and body types. 59. Economic structure.

60. Political structure. 61. Communal structure. 62. Religious structure. 63. Labour structure. 64. Educational structure. 65. Demand-supply in crimino-economics. 66. Input-output in crimino-economics. 67. Desire to have social mobility. 68. Convictions to commit crimes. 69. Tolerance to crimes.

70. Criminals and crimes are parts of the society 71. Criminal as a product of the society. 72. Crime as a human act and a social fact. 73. Imperfection in society and/or social life. 74. Social pathology. 75. Expression of originality, necessity of social functioning. 76. Creative genius of the crime-doer. 77. Necessity for social evolution for social dynamism, change in laws. 78. Reaction to frustration causing situation, expression of aggression to frustration creating situations/environments. 79. Reaction to experiences to problems.

80. Association with crime-doers having same/similar personality desires and aptitude. 81. Interaction with crime-doers of same/similar crime tendencies, wishes and attitudes. 82. Expertise in committing crimes. 83. Self-confidence to commit crimes. 84. Incarceration to penal institutions. 85. Reaction to punitive laws and punishments. 86. Custodial nature of prison life and reaction to such confinements. 87. Recidivism. 88. Influence of the same/similar environments which are crime prone. 89. Influence of a criminal society.

90. Society's reluctance to punish the guilty. 91. Hypocricy in dealing with the crime-doers. 92. Instincts and reaction to instincts. 93. Cultural exchange. 94. Sub-cultural interchange. 95. Media and mini-screens. 96. Films and T.V. serials. 97. Criminal motivations and media influence. 98. Sub-cultural (Criminal) influence. 99. Material and non-material culture.

100. Failure of the value system. 101. Conflict between material and non-material culture. 102. Culture conflicts. 103. Failure to have meaningful methods to combat crimes. 104. No police surveillance. 105. Failure of police shadowing. 106. Human ecology and its impact. 107. Breakdown of the usual institutional methods to control crimes. 108. Poor community and area. 109. Urbanization and urban life.

110. Vertical and horizontal mobility. 111. Cultural lag. 112. Crime as a byproduct of human ecology. 113. Inadequacy of punishments. 114. Co-existence of crime and punishment. 115. No deterrent effect of punishments. 116. No meaningful or effective punishment. 117. Justification/rationalization for committing crimes. 118. Inadequate penal laws and their

museum piece nature. 119. Easy escape from the clutches of law and law enforcement machinery.

120. No detection in many criminal cases. 121. No conviction to crime-doers. 122. Failure of the prosecution machinery. 123. Accusatorial system of criminal justice administration. 124. Inquisitorial system of criminal justice administration. 125. Social milieu and crime causation. 126. Learning and mixing with people having similar tendencies. 127. Communication and transferring of the knowledge and know-how of committing crimes. 128. Chances to escape from being caught. The more the chances, the more will be the involvement in the commission of crimes. 129. Low grade intelligence, mental retardation, mental deficiency.

130. Low I.Q. 131. Reduced power to judge the nature of the criminal act. 132. Inability to differentiate good and bad. 133. Muscle power. 134. Money power. 135. Mind power. 136. Short stay in prisons and its ineffectiveness. 137. Contacts with crime-doers. 138. Influence of alcohol and drugs. 139. Urge to commit crimes.

140. Encouragement to commit crimes. 141. Slum life. 142. Obscene literature. 143. Morphology. 144. Insanity proper. 145. Psychoneurosis. 146. Coercion to commit crimes. 147. Weak mental structure. 148. Victims of crime. 149. Authority and authoritarian attitude.

150. Authoritarian ego. 151. Ill-gotten money. 152. Ill-captured positions. 153. Exercise of pseudo-authority. 154. Misuse of Power. 155. Abuse of power. 156. Jealousy. 157. Inferiority feeling. 158. Legal system. 159. Sub-culture of criminality.

160. Criminal culture. 161. Lawyer criminals. 162. Police officer criminals. 163. Inadeque formation of super-ego. 164. Excessive 'Id' complexes. 165. Denial of justice. 166. Mishandling of offenders. 167. Lack of opportunities to live like a law abiding citizen. 168. Crime producing situations. 169. Police leniency to crime and criminals.

170. Instability of the social order. 171. Failure in police vigilance. 172. Poor schooling. 173. Defects in educational system. 174. Physically deteriorated areas. 175. Disorganized

areas in cities. 176. Migration. 177. Dislocation of population. 178. City culture. 179. Urban anonymity.

180. Emotional instability. 181. No guilt feelings. 182. Imporper handling of juvenile delinquents. 183. Family history of crimes. 184. Antiquated criminal laws. 185. Regionalism. 186. Linguistic differences. 187. Parochialism. 188. Racism. 189. Casteism and subcasteism.

190. Terrorist attitude. 191. Extremist tendencies. 192. Fundamentalism. 193. Fanaticism. 194. Insurgency. 195. Social alienation. 196. A "criminal after all" attitude and approach. 197. Human rights activists and people who assume such roles. 198. Deception in police work. 199. Dishonesty in justice administration.

200. Inducement to commit crimes. 201. Low visibility in crime control, reduction and prevention. 202. Preparedness to suffer the consequence/s of the commission of a crime. 203. Bureaucratic coverage for the crime committed. 204. Justification and rationalizations for the ill-doings committed by vested interests. 205. Organizational support. 206. No official reaction to the crimes committed. 207. Official lethargy and inaction towards the commission of crimes. 208. No public reactions to the crimes. 209. People's/official inability, fear, weakness to react against crimes.

210. Organized forces (communal, labour, student, political forces) and their collective strength. 211. Equality of sexes and women's parity with men. 212. Crime as a way of life (For most of the businessmen, politicians, bureaucrats, members of crime syndicates, *pujaris* and some of the prayermen). 213. Love-hate relationship with crime and criminal acts. 214. Violating law for observance of law. 215. Failure of the unofficial machinery (Home, School, Religious Institution etc.) to control and reduce crimes. 216. Strong determination to commit crimes. 217. Problem families. 218. Growth in transport and communication. 219. Animality in man.

220. Uselessness of the prison trades taught to the inmates. 221. Need and greed for wealth, position, status and acceptance. 222. Personality maladjustments and sickness. 223. Psychoses and grave mental disorders. 224. Becoming master of a

situation. 225. Performing as the servant of a situation. 226. Becoming the victim of a situation. 227. Social inducement to deviant behaviour. 228. Violence prone mind and sub-culture of violence. 229. Criminal sub-culture (Tribes).

230. Respectability given to crimes. 231. Acquisitive urges and remuneration offered by crimes. 232. Underworld criminal culture. 233. Upper world criminal culture. 234. Underhand dealing with power, authority and criminals. 235. God, gods, goddesses, god's instigation, godly thoughts and human weakness. 236. Divinities, divine compulsions, deities, god-men, human gods, incarnations of god. 237. Prayer and prayerism, prayer addiction. 238. Professionalism. 239. Expertism.

240. Divine curse. 241. Piety and piety addiction. 242. Gambling and gambling addiction. 243. Cop mentality. 244. God mentality and ritualism. 245. Instinctual satisfaction. 246. Drive reduction. 247. Hedonism. 248. Epicurianism. 249. Economic structure.

250. *Mafia* mind. 251. Avarice. 252. Crime syndicate attitude. 253. Self-assertion drives. 254. Acquisitiveness-mind. 255. Culture conscience. 256. Ethnic structure. 257. Rivalry. 258. Gang-unity. 259. Linguistic structure.

260. Religious structure. 261. Socio-economic conditions. 262. Atavism. 263. Physical anomalies. 264. Imitation. 265. Identification. 266. Suggestion. 267. Constituational, physical and mental aspects. 268. Inherited predisposition. 269. Inheritance of criminality.

270. Temperament. 271. Congenital conditions. 272. Glandular functioning and misfunctioning. 273. Endocrine malfunctioning. 274. Body mind types as asthenic, athletic and pyknic. 275. Anomie in society. 276. Breaking down of social control. 277. Chromosomal abnormality. 278. Stubbornness. 279. Gang culture and group autonomy.

280. Sibling rivalry. 281. Gang rivalry. 282. Conflicts of conduct norms. 283. Lack of guilt feeling. 284. Culture conflicts. 285. Differential association. 286. Training. 287. Self-concept. 288. Adjustment conflicts. 289. Extroversion-Introversion. 290. Conditioning and 291. Doctrine of easy money-making.

I stop here my search for the etiology of crime. Anyway, I am not inclined to accept the theory of **causality** to explain why do people commit crimes. The reason is that there are millions and millions of crimes and precisely therefore there cannot be any scope for a theory of causality.

THEORY OF CAUSATION OF CRIMES

Multiple causation approach is accepted by some criminologists. In other words, there cannot be a single cause for a crime. O.K., let there be a multitude of causes. To their views, I add my views and according to me, the causes may be—

- (i) Known to self and others
- (ii) Known to self and not to others
- (iii) Known to others and not to self
- (iv) Unknown to self and unknown to others.

Therefore, I may emphatically say that there is no meaning in spekaing about the causes of crime rather, there is the scope for talking about the causative factors of crime. In any case, one cannot enumerate all the causative factors behind the commission of crimes. Hence, there is scope only for a **theory of causation** and not at all for a **theory of causality.**

In 1998 when I authored **Crime, Police and Correction,** I wrote:

- (i) *Crimes are of different types—biological, psychological, financial, political, communal or any such. The causes for each type may be many and different from one another.*
- (ii) *White collar crimes, Blue collar crimes, No collar crimes, Khaki-collar crimes..... conventional criminality, convictional criminality, enforcement criminality..... cognizable crimes, organized crimes, political crimes, economic crimes, socio-economic crimes.... and thus crimes are of many kinds and varieties.*

(iii) *No man konws clearly what motivates him to commit a crime in a particular way. There are conscious and unconscious forces operating in every crime-doer. Likewise, there are many environmental factors operating upon him.*

(iv) *Multitude of factors of different kinds may be responsible for causing crimes and delinquency. Many of such factors are beyond the control of individuals living in a society—and they include the police, prosecutors, judges and the judicial system. Corporate crimes are criminal acts of corporations and individuals acting in their corporate capacity.*

JEL crimes, Nexus crimes, consensus crimes, bureaucratic crimes, sweet heart crimes, grass-eater crimes, mosquito crimes, shark crimes, meat-eater crimes, suite crimes, slum crimes, enforcement crimes, international crimes, trafficking, racketeering, net-work crimes, cyber crimes, *Mafia,* crime syndicates, charity crimes, war crimes, extremism, fundamentalism, fanaticism, terrorism, insurgency, religious bigotry, crimes by human gods, (so named or so claimed incarnations of god), business crimes, money chain, multi-marketing, internet crimes, financing and investment frauds, insurance crimes, media crimes, politician's crimes, criminalization of politics, politicization of criminals, policization of criminals, administration of less justice or wounded justice, miscarriage of justice, corruption and malpractices, flesh trade and pornography, traditional crimes like murder, rape etc. waste justice delivery etc. are crimes for which the causative factors may be many, various and different. No one on earth will be able to say why people commit crimes of different types and nature. It is indeed difficult or rather impossible to specify the specific causative factors of crime here.

To quote again from my book **Contemporary Indian Criminology**—

"Why do the people involve in the commission of all these or similar crimes? Researches show that crimes are, perhaps, one of the few things which need not be taught to people. For, they learn

themselves to commit various types of crimes if they get opportunities. According to me, there is something in man and it makes him to commit crimes. This "something" cannot be different from what the animals have. They too have "something" which activates them to do a thing. Hence, the "something" seen common in man and animals may be/are the instincts in animals and drives in man". I explain my theory, i.e., **Push-pull-ego factor** theory in detail in the chapters that follow.

Coming to a particular type of crime—say, *Mafia* crime—we may see a variety of people involved. What works as a cause of crime in all those involved in the commission of such a crime? The *Mafia* may be regional, national or international and it is not just possible to identify and earmark the causative factors operating in each and everyone involved in *Mafia* crimes. The same is the position in nexus crimes, organized crimes, crime syndicates, racketeering and international trafficking of drugs, human trafficking, cyber crimes, net-work offences, corporate crimes etc. and it is so because there are a number of people involved in the criminal activities. What about the political crimes?—about white collar crimes? about terrorism and insurgency? What to say about communal riots and religious bigotry? What about crimes by trade unions and insurance companies? My surveys on the causative or etiological aspects of crime and criminals convince me that the researchers have been concerned only with individual crimes in which only a single person is found to be guilty of the crime he/she has committed. They were interested to identify individual murder cases, rape cases, kidnapping cases, forgery and misappropriation of property etc. which one might see in penal codes enacted during nineteenth century or earlier. At that time, criminology was not even born and researchers were concerned only with administration of **criminal justice** and nothing more. Today, one sees social justice, equal justice, victim justice, gender justice, economic justice, human rights justice, administrative justice, domestic justice, correctional justice, political justice, holistic justice, juvenile justice and justice to the old, the infirm and the handicapped, democratic justice, judicial justice, justice to the justice system etc. In such a changed situation, identifying the causative aspects of crime becomes difficult if not impossible. I find **Push-pull-ego factor** Theory to be the most suitable one to explain the etiology of crime and criminal behaviour.

DICTIONARY: CRIMES AND CRIMINAL BEHAVIOUR

I took Webster's English Dictionary and some words (adjectives and nouns) having relevance or importance to explaining and understanding human behaviour were taken note of. For example, take the word **criminal** and find out adjectives or nouns to give meanings to C,R,I,M,I,N,A,L and thus one may put—

C	—Courteous	*(Courtesy)*	..... ×	Discourteous
R	—Reasonable	*(Reasonableness, reasonability)*	.... ×	Unreasonable
I	—Irrational	*(Irrationalism, irrationality)*	.... ×	Rational
M	—Malicious	*(Maliciousness)*	.... ×	Non-malicious
I	—Industrious	*(Industriousness)*	.... ×	Non-industrious
N	—Nasty	*(Nastiness)*	....×.....	Non-nasty
L	—Lovable	*(Lovableness)*	.... ×	Non-lovable

What about 'A' – Second last but one in CRIMINAL.

It means that every adjective or noun has an opposite in the same ***dictionary***. For example, the letter C has *courteous* (courtesy), *careful* (carefulness), *co-operative* (co-operation). *Courteous* has discourteous, *careful* has careless and *co-operative* has non-co-operative as opposites in the same *Dictionary*. *Courteous, Careful, Co-operative,* as well as Discourteous, Careless and Non-co-operative qualify human behaviour or explain how the behaviour is. While *'courteous'* is positive, the 'discourteous' is negative. Likewise, *'careful'* is positive and the 'careless' is negative. Thus, one may see the positive and negative aspects of human behaviour. The words which give **"positive"** meanings show the nature of human behaviour as **"non-criminal"**. The words which give **"negative"** meanings tell about the nature of human behaviour as **"criminal"**. The same approach can be taken to all letters in the word **"criminal"**. In other words too, the Dictionary has equal number of **"positive"** adjectives (nouns) and **"negative"** adjectives (nouns). Hence, the **Push-pull-ego factor** Theory assumes—

1. ***For every positive act, there is an equal and opposite act which is negative in return.***
2. ***The positive acts and the equal and opposite negative acts in return make the society dynamic and thus it moves on.***
3. ***Good acts/omissions and bad acts/omissions are almost equal in any society at a given time. This keeps the equilibrium of the society.***

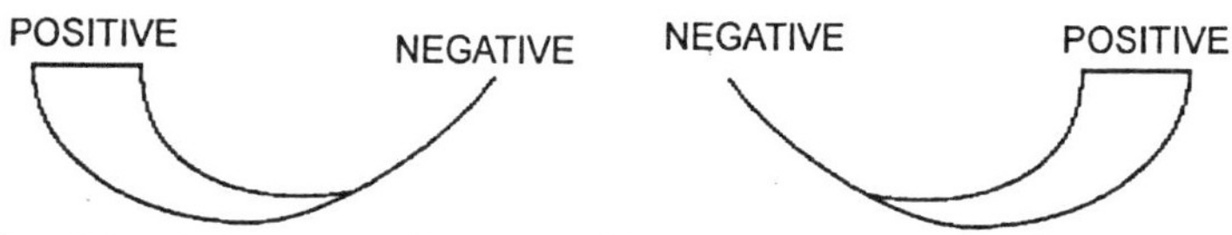

Fig. 1.1: Acts move from positive to negative and *vice versa*
Omissions move from positive to negative and *vice versa*

The good acts/omissions (positive) in society are not of ten taken note of by majority of the people while bad (negative) acts/omissions are taken serious or very serious note of by many (all) people and some times, they become news in the media. This means that crimes are noticed and many good acts (not crimes) go unnoticed. This is the reason why crimes become a topic of discussion among the people, media and a talk in the town. Good acts/actions walk slowly and bad acts/actions fly at light-speed.

I do not find any man with only positive qualities. Similarly, no one is seen with only negative qualities. Everyone is a

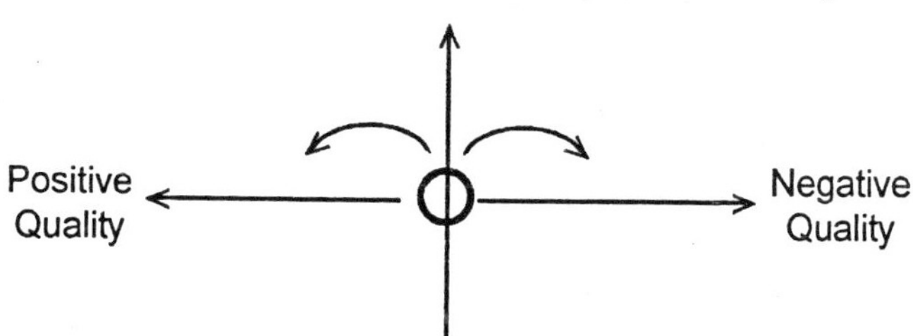

Fig. 1.2: Equilibrium of positive and negative energy.

mixture of both in his thoughts, words, acts/omissions. The positive and negative energy of the man is having a tug of war and it maintains the equilibrium so long as the positive and negative forces are equal in strength. If it is not, then the equilibrium is disturbed and eventually broken.

Equilibrium is maintained so long as the energy is equal and opposite. Every moment in a man's life, this tug of war is going on and he tries to maintain the equilibrium. This is true in the case of any society. This is what I mean when I speak about the **Quota theory of crime** and **Criminal behaviour.**

QUOTA THEORY OF CRIME AND CRIMINAL BEHAVIOUR

Every society has a quota of crimes/criminal behaviour just like every society has a quota of good behaviour (non-criminal acts/omissions). A society needs such a quota for its existence, survival, progress and development. A man does many good acts just like he does bad acts. A few of the good acts may be noticed and similarly, a few of the bad acts will be unnoticed. Many are ignored and some are forgotten. **Push-pull-ego factor approach** elaborates this further in the chapers that follow.

Every individual has **push factors** just like every group of individuals has them. Every community, sect, denomination, caste, sub-caste, race, culture, sub-culture has **push factors.** Every society has **push factors.** The whole humanity has **push factors.** Every individual, group, community, sect has **pull factors.** Finally, every individual has an **ego factor** just like every group, community, caste, race has the **ego factor.** Hence, I expose the **Push-pull-ego factor** approach to explain all sorts of crimes in very many descriptions.

PREDISPOSING CAUSES AND PRECIPITATING CAUSES

A word about the predisposing causes (Factors) and precipitating causes (Factors) become necessary before we proceed further in our pursuit for the formation of **Push-pull-ego factor** theory. When I studied a variety of crimes—both official and unofficial— I found that in many cases there were predisposing[3] causes. Hence, I wrote:

> *"What are the principal factors which influence a person to commit crimes? At least, one may see four factors in any specific case. They are—(i) the predisposing factors, (ii) the precipitating factors[4], (iii) the contributory[5] factors and (iv) factors present but not apparently found operative."*

I wrote further: *"Police officers, prosecutors, judges and prison officials cannot see all these push and pull factors unless they are properly trained in behavioural sciences and are open to appreciate the behavioural dynamics"* (see, **Crime, Police and Correction**). A person generally does not commit a crime one day too soon. Criminologists make use of **case-study** methods to find out the factors which operated in an individual from early infancy and their impact and influence to make him/her a crime-doer or a criminal later. For this, his/her family organization and nature, relations and interactions, religious training, financial position, economic background, leisure-time activities, educational foundation, moral and spiritual training etc. are studied in depth. This is highly needed in the case of recidivists who repeat the commission of crimes even after the institutional treatment and correction. Today, the objective of punishment has come to "development of personality in an upright way in the right direction". Forget about the earlier promoted and propagated objectives of incarceration.

I have interviewed children in institutions for juveniles who had conflict with law. I found that some of them hailed from disorganized families without having any values. There was no social commitment for them and I found that they had a very fertile land for criminality to prosper and progress. A bullock cart or a bufallow cart driver may not have a house to stay. They may have overcrowded families or theirs may be an unemployed or under employed family. No time for responsible parenting, mothering and mother's care, no proper schooling and all opportunities to have the company of bad children including notorious criminals and bandits of all descriptions. The predisposing factors to commit crimes in such instances may be very conducive to become a crime-doer later. Hence, I wrote:

(1) *It has been noticed that truancy and vagrancy among children become pre-delinquency stages of their involvement in the commission of crime.*
(2) *A sub-culture of criminality in the family, group or society may work as a predisposing cause for committing crimes. The criminal tribes (now, they are called denotified tribes) in India do have a sub-culture of criminality.*

Those having a predisposing background and personality profile are, if provided with precipitating climate, likely to involve in the commission of crimes. A sudden provocation may ignite a crime in some people. It is like fire to crackers. There is a Malayalam saying about women: "Earlier a fragile person and now a pregnant one." It is like that. Those who have predisposing factors when provided with precipitating factors, they become crime doers[6] or criminals[7] as the case may be.

PRE-DISPOSING, PRECIPITATING, CONTRIBUTORY AND FACTORS PRESENT BUT NOT APPARENTLY FOUND OPERATIVE

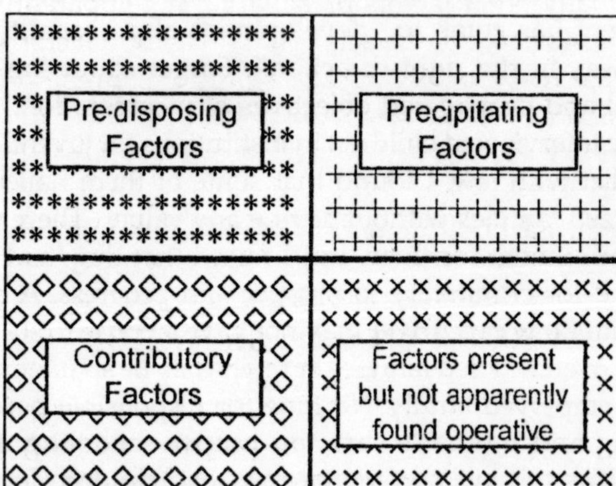

Fig. 1.3: Pre-disposing, Precipitating, Contributory and Factors Present but not apparently found operative.

What are the precipitating factors—

(i) to hasten the occurrence of a crime?
(ii) to bring about prematurely, hastily or suddenly the commission of a crime?

In the commission of a crime, the precipitating factors have a lot of influence. Birds of the same feathers flock together and thus people who have the pre-disposing factors gather together. This is seen in *Mafia*, money-chain, multi-marketing, investment frauds, organized crimes, black marketing etc. They will look for precipitating factors and when they find them, they may involve in the commission of all kinds of nefarious activities. Hospital *Mafia*, liquor *Mafia*, insurance *Mafia*, automobile *Mafia*, flat *Mafia*, tourism *Mafia*, sex-*Mafia* and thus the list is limitless. All those who have pre-disposing factors commit all sorts of crimes when they find precipitating factors. "Strike the iron when it is hot"—is the approach. A weak physical body is likely to catch many diseases.

There may be any number of contributory factors for the promotion of crimes. The nexus among the political leaders, bureaucrats, businessmen and favourable climate to commit the crimes with immunity may be a contributory factor. There may be many other factors present, but not apparently found operative. *Vis major* or the acts of God may be a factor which is not apparently found operative, but is present for the commission of certain crimes.

The best approach or strategy taken is to reduce or culminate the conditions likely to develop criminal personality in children. Early childhood training has an important role here.

DEVELOPMENT OF PUSH FACTORS IN CRIMINALITY

The **Push factors** are— (1) Animality, (2) Spirituality, (3) Morality/Ethics, and (4) Intelligence. As said elsewhere, animality consists of Instincts, Spirituality consists of Faith and

Belief, Morality/Ethics consists of Guilt or No Guilt feeling and Intelligence consists of (i) Memory, (ii) Expansion, (iii) Comprehension, (iv) Critical analysis, and (v) Intuitiveness/creativity/inventiveness.

How do they develop? They develop if and only if facilitating environments [precipitating, contributory etc.] are given. A seed develops into a huge tree if it is given proper environment. If the environment is negative for development, it dies out. Again, take the example of human eyes. They develop and see light and colours only if they are provided with light. If the child lives in complete darkness, the eyes do not develop and they cannot see light. Similarly—

1. Spirituality: Man has the potency and it develops only when adequate facilities are provided. For example—

(i) If one wants to have a Christian child, provide environments for developing Christian values. If the child should have Catholic faith, then give the facility for that. Likewise, one may grow as a Muslim, Hindu, Jain, Sikh or Jew **(FAITH).**

(ii) If you want to have a rationalist, humanist, agnostic, atheist to grow, provide such environments. One can plant, nourish and develop superstition is as well. There are people who have belief in devils, in nature's strength, in imaginary beings, in wild animals, birds, reptiles, in rituals, in *'isms'*, *'ologies'*, *'sophies'* etc. **(BELIEF).** They are the **Pull factors.**

2. Morality and Ethics: Man has the potency for ethical and/or moral development. This contains the rules, laws, traditions, customs etc. which form human conscience—the *super ego*—the *Do's and Don'ts—the Dictates* of a human mind uprightly formed in the right direction. When violations are found, then he feels guilty for it. If the environments **(pull factors)** are bad/unfavourable, then no guilt feelings will be there if at all the rules, laws etc. are violated. Morality is universal and ethics is individualistic.

3. Animality: Provide facilitating environment for each instinct to develop in a desirable way—in an upright way—in the right direction. If cruelty is to be developed, provide environments for the development of cruelty. If aggression is to be developed, provide environments for the development of aggression. Good mothering, good schooling, good media, good friendship etc. will be good **pull factors** for the development of instinctual potencies in an upright way in the right direction.

4. Intelligence: Man has the potency for intellectual development. It is for this purpose, education is provided. Education is not only for academic achievements. There is the moral education, religious education, cultural education, ethical education and thus the character formation is ensured. Family, Schools, Colleges, Religion, Media, Exhortations—all are important in character formation and intellectual achievements. A **total** man is to be formed and the *holistic* man is formed owing to an interaction between the **Push** and **pull** factors. If the **Pull** factors are favourable, a scientist or an inventor can be created. If the **Pull** factors are bad and crime-creating, then a criminal, say a terrorist, a Naxalite, a *Mafia* king, a white collar criminal, a corrupt man can be resulted.

The Chapters that follow will illustrate further the working and interaction of **Push** and **pull** forces to make an **Ego factor** to commit crimes in society.

Notes

1. One of the minute, usually actively motile gametes in semen, which serve to fertilize the ovum (*The Random House College Dictionary*).
2. In Theology, the supreme spirit of evil, SATAN; a subordinate evil spirit at enmity with God and having power to afflict humans both with bodily disease and with spiritual corruption (Webster's).
3. Predisposing means "to give an inclination or tendency to beforehand, make, susceptible: *Genetic factors may predispose human beings to certain metabolic diseases.* [Webster's]"

4. Precipitating means "to hasten the occurrence of, hastily or suddenly."
5. Contributory means furnishing something toward a result (Webster's).
6. A crime-doer means a person who violates a law (any kind) but not taken note of by others.
7. A criminal means a person who has violated a law (any kind) but taken note of by others.

2
Individual, Group and Society

Individuals commit crimes and therefore individuals are punished. In the Indian Penal Code–1860 (Any Penal Codes), one sees, perhaps, dacoity, i.e., *"When five or more persons conjointly commit or attempt to commit robbery, or where the whole number of persons conjointly committing or attempting to commit a robbery and persons present and aiding such commission or attempt, amount to five or more, every person so committing, attempting or aiding, is said to commit dacoity."*

This may be the only crime in which a group of people involved in the commission of crime is punished in India. There is also a section on ***criminal conspiracy*** which reads:

"When two or more persons agree to do, or cause to be done—

(1) an illegal act; or
(2) an act which is not illegal by illegal means, such an agreement is designated a criminal conspiracy provided that no agreement except an agreement to commit an offence shall amount to a criminal conspiracy unless some act besides the agreeemnt is done by one or more parties to such agreement in pursuance thereof.

Explanation

It is immaterial whether the illegal act is the ultimate object of such agreement, or is merely incidental to that object."

The criminal justice system keeps an **individual** at the centre and the police, prosecutors, defence counsels, media, public, courts and the centres of personality development (formerly, the prisons, centres of correction) and after-care services are functioning around him/her for transforming him/her or reforming him/her to be a law abiding citizen. No one seems to be concerned with a group or society as none of them is seen to be keen in converting the group or society to be law abiding. Even in countries where **criminal tribes** existed, the justice system (the sub-systems involved in it) appeared to be concerned only with individual offenders. Of course, one sees in religious texts that an entire group or community or society was punished for having committed crimes. In the **Old Testament,** one reads:

"Yahweh saw that the wickedness of man was great on the earth, and that the thoughts in his heart fashioned nothing, but the wickedness all day long. Yahweh regretted having made man on the earth and his heart grieved. I will rid the earth's face of man, my own creation. Yehweh said and of animals also, reptiles too, and the birds of heaven; for I regret having made them."

This is the story of Noah:

> Noah was a good man, a man of integrity among his contemporaries and he walked with God. Noah became the father of three sons, Shem, Ham and Japheth. The earth grew corrupt in God's sight, and filled with violence. God contemplated the earth: it was corrupt, for corrupt were the ways of all flesh on the earth.

PREPARATION FOR THE FLOOD

God said to Noah, "The end has come for all things of flesh; I have decided this, because the earth is full of violence of man's making and I will efface them from the earth....

For my part I mean to bring a flood, and send the waters over the earth, to destroy all flesh on it, every living creature under heaven, everything on earth shall perish...

For in seven days time I mean to make it rain on earth for forty days and nights, and I will rid, the earth of every living thing that I made... And so all things of flesh perished that moved on the earth, birds, cattle, wild beasts, everything that swarms on the earth, and every man.... (*The Old Testament: Genesis* 6:5-22; 7:1-14, *The Jerusalem Bible*, Darton, Longman & Todd, London, 1966)".

Again, we see the destruction of Sodom and we read: *"....Yahweh rained on Sodom and Gomorrah brimstone and fire from Yahweh. He overthrew these towns and the whole plain, with all the inhabitants of the towns, and everything that grew there...."* (*The Old Testament: Genesis* : 19: 23-26).

Today, one sees individuals committing crimes—sins, vices, immoral acts, amoral acts, offences, anti-social acts and violations of many rules, laws, regulations, customs and traditions which are culturally transmitted from generations to generations and hence, I wrote:

(1) *"For the psychologists, a crime is an expression of a maladjusted personality and what is required is to help the maladjusted to make proper adjustments. A change in the personality of the criminal is what is required and not the destruction of the criminal's personality."*

(2) *"People wrote books on crime and criminals. Sometimes they become best sellers. This is an honour given to individual criminals who become successful in their activities. No doubt there is an appreciation for what the criminals do although there may be a disapproval of what they have done."*

(3) *"A mother punishes her child, so that, it may be corrected. The same principle is true whenever a person commits a crime in society. The society punishes him/her to correct the violator of law."*

(4) *"A person commits crime because he thinks that he can escape from being caught"* (*See,* **Crime, Police and Correction**).

Today one sees a group or community committing crimes and such crimes include in these days—(1) white collar crimes, (2) nexus crimes, (3) organized crimes, (4) *Mafia* crimes, (5) JEL crimes, (6) crime syndicates and racketeering, (7) enforcement crimes and corruption, (8) burcaucratic crimes and malpractices, (9) corporate crimes, etc. As they are latecomers, they are not well defined in the antique penal codes which are centuries old museum pieces. The groups—i.e., the members comprising in the group—commit crimes and hence, I worte:

(1) *"Crimes in the Indian Penal Code-1860 are indeed old. The new manifestations of the old crimes are seen and the problem is that one cannot fit the new patterns of crime in the old definitions as seen in the Code which was enacted about one and half a century back."*

(2) *"Price-rigging has a corrosive effect on the moral standards by which Indian business is conducted. The businessmen defraud their customers. Bribery is a cancer in Indian social life. The Government employees exploit their official position to the advantage of those who offer illegal gratification. Corruption is a way of life for many politicians and top lovel bureaucrats and it has a threatening effect in the financial stability and economic growth of the country. In thc background of all these syndicate-white collar-political-bureaucratic-business-economic-religious-social crimes, what is after all a simple theft? a simple hurt?"*

(3) *"Most successful crimes today arc not detected by police and today reported crimes remain unsolved by the police".*

(4) *"Bureaucratic coverage for the crimes the members of bureaucracy commit is indeed shocking. The bureaucratic coverage can produce a variety of criminological responses including corruption, concoction, manipulation, misappropriation etc. The bureaucratic system prevailing in any society protects the corrupt, exploitative, illegal and unfair interests of thc bureacratic community"* (*See* **Crime, Police and Correction**).

Today one sees a society as a whole committing crimes and such crimes include: (1) terrorism, extremism, fundamentalism, fanaticism, insurgency; (2) communal riots and religious bigotry; (3) casteism, sub-casteism and racialism;

(4) political fights and wars; and (5) student agitations and agrarian unrest etc. and hence, I wrote:

(1) *"Look into the characteristics of the social milieu more than the characteristics of the individual criminal to understand crime and criminal behaviour."*

(2) *"Political crimes are not crimes committed by politicians. In fact, they are not defined in any penal statutes today. Treason, sedition, espionage, other acts endangering the external security of the State, rebellion and incitement to civil war are all viewed as offences exclusively against the sovereign authority and are considered as pure political offences."* (Kittie & Vadackumchery)

(3) *"Offences that endanger the life and property of individuals but are carried out in connection with and in furtherance of a crime against the State are called complex or connected to political offences."*

(4) *"Communal forces, labour forces, student forces, political forces—and thus the organized forces—can afford to commit crimes with some immunity. Likewise, the police forces also can commit crimes with some immunity—say research studies. "People who commit crimes are often individuals and as such they cannot claim immunity for the acts they do just like people in organized groups enjoy. One and the same act committed by a person individually and by a person being a member of the organized group is viewed differently. Correspondingly, crimes become no crimes when they are committed by organized groups"* (*See*, **Crime, Police and Correction**).

CRIME CAUSATION FOR INDIVIDUAL, GROUP AND SOCIETY: THE THEORY

In the previous chapter, I exposed my theory of **Push-pull-ego factor** approach. There, I brought out the **Animal Mind (Ego), Intellectual Mind (Ego), Spiritual Mind (Ego), Moral/ Ethical Mind (Ego)** as the **Push factors.** Each **Mind** or **Ego** will be extensively dealt with in the chapters that follow. Nevertheless, I want to bring out the importance of—

(1) Individual Mind: Push Factors and Pull factors

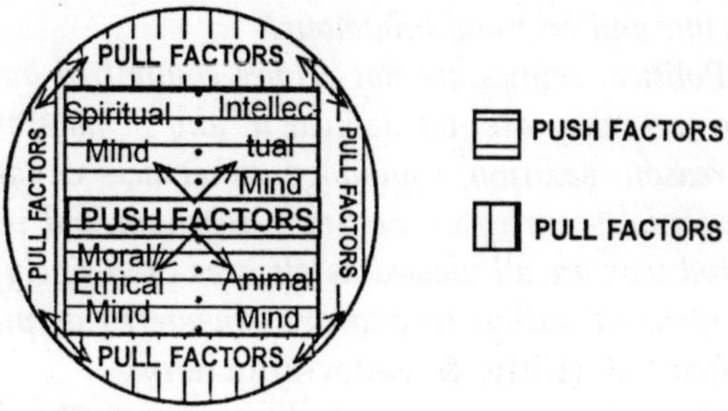

Fig. 2.1: Individual Mind.

(2) Group Mind: Push Factors-Pull Factors

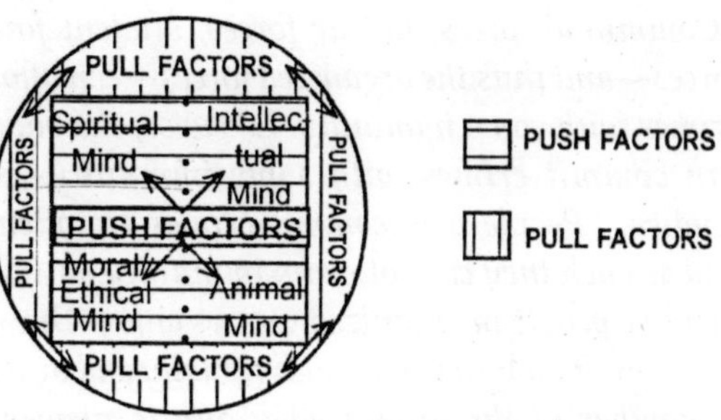

Fig. 2.2: Group Mind.

(3) Society Mind: Push Factors-Pull factors

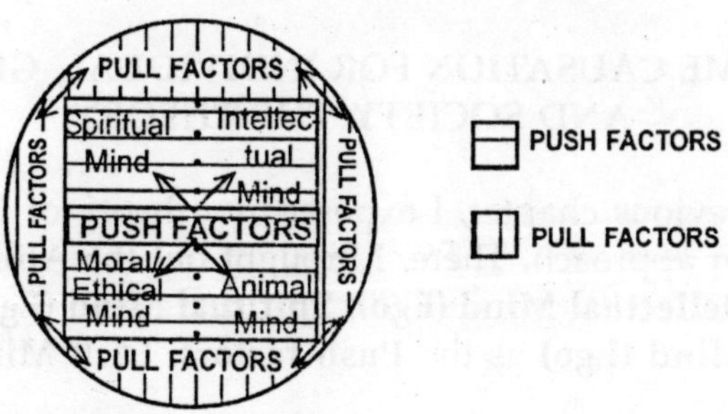

Fig. 2.3: Society Mind.

Individual Mind (Ego), Group Mind (Ego) and Society Mind (Ego): the formation will be as under.

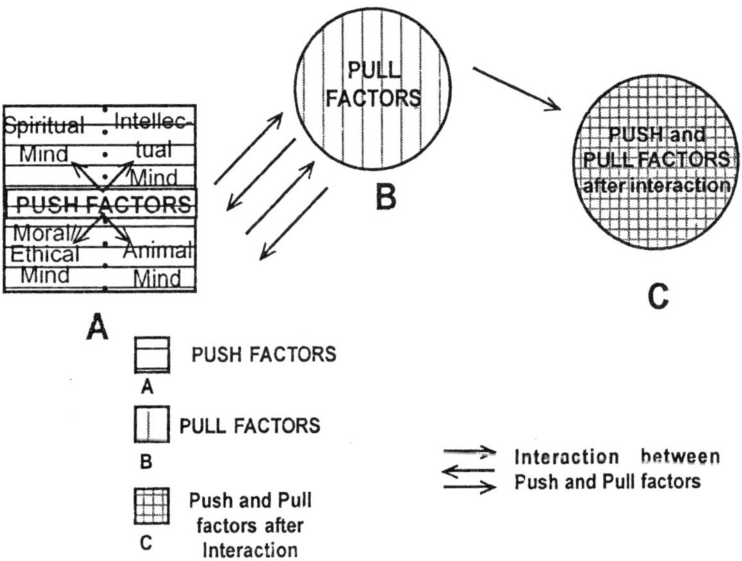

Fig. 2.4: Melted or amalgamated individual ego, group ego, society ego after push and pull interactions.

The **amalgamated individual group, society mind (Ego)** are formed out of the interactions between the **push** and **pull** factors. In other words = $\frac{\text{Pull Factors}}{\text{Push Factors}} \div$

and/or **Pull Factors × Push Factors**

In my book **Contemporary Indian Criminology**, I have said: "an interaction between **push** and **pull factors** means that a man (Group or Society) can survive only by fighting and/or interacting with his (their) environments. In other words, it is algebraically put—

$$\text{C.B.} = \frac{\text{Pull Factors}}{\text{Push Factors}} \div \qquad \text{...(1)}$$

C.B. = **Pull Factor × Push Factor** ... (2)

Where C.B. = **Criminal Behaviour.** Whenever, the **pull factors** and **push factors** interact either by fighting [as shown in (1)] or by co-operating [as shown in (2)], a value is obtained. The **mind** with this value is called the **Ego.** The C above is the **individual ego or group ego or society ego.**

GROUP MIND (EGO)

The **Group Mind (Ego)** too will be just like the **individual mind (Ego).** The **animality, spirituality, morality/ethics and intelligence** will be for a group (formed on the basis of religion, faith, "*...ologies*", "*...isms*" etc.). A Group has the same animal instincts just like an individual has. For example—Take the instinct called **escape.** Whenever a danger is perceived, the individuals escape by running away from the danger. Likewise, a group too does the same thing in the same way. What happens during a natural calamity? Coming to the commission of crime, a group as a single force will attack people as one may notice in the crime of dacoity, communal fights, liguistic or regional disputes or racial conflicts.

The animal instinct of **acquisitiveness** is expressed in *Mafia* or similar organized crimes. Hence, it is rightly called the crimes of **greed.** The group may resort to mass killings and thus we see *grenade-crimes* which the terrorist groups often resort to. The animal instinct of **food seeking** may be seen in mass scale lootings and arson by groups. The animal instinct of **self-assertion** will be noticed in "*kudipaka*" [i.e., mutual rivalry] among various gangs involved in the commission of crimes.

In **group ego,** one may find that the Animality (instinct) overpowering the **spirituality, morality/ethics** and **intelligence** and an interaction with the **pull factors** around the group makes them to form the ***Group Ego.*** Every group, i.e., the criminal gangs, the dacoits, the terrorists, the white collar criminals, gangs, the *Mafia*—will have to see a lot of realities for forming a **Group Ego.**

SOCIETY EGO

I remember the words used by Martin Luther King, the African American leader in USA and he said, *"I have a dream....... I have a dream..... one day........ and certainly"* a **society ego** was created by such a speech. The animal instincts among the **black** could be grouped together to form a **Society Ego.** Mark Antony, in Shakespeare, said: *"The Fire will work now"* and it meant that the animal instinct would work as a **Society Ego** then. What happens among the suppressed communities? They fight together and they involve in the commission of various crimes one after another. In liberation—struggles, people in a society express their animal instinct in unison and they always proclaim *"United we stand, Divided we fall"*. A **Society Ego** becomes necessary for obtaining success in life—and so is the case with criminal activities. What happens in wars? Hence, **Society Ego** too is just like **individual ego** and **group ego** for the commission of crimes.

HOW DO THE EGO FORM?

How do the **Push** and **Pull** Factors interact to form the **Egos** have been discussed above. An **Ego** (Individual, group or society) with the dominance of an instinct, or with the dominance of more than one instinct is shown in Fig. 2.5.

Fig. 2.5 shows how does a particular animal instinct is seen dominating in an **Individual Ego, Group Ego or Society Ego.**

Illustrations

1. **An Individual Ego** with the dominance of the instinct called **curiosity** will involve in various kinds of investment frauds, visa rackets, false employment bureaus etc.
2. A **Group Ego** with the dominance of the instinct called **acquisitiveness** will involve in various kinds of schemes to cheat the people. If the group has pugnacity as the dominant instinct, the **group ego** will form a gang or *Mafia* to amass wealth.

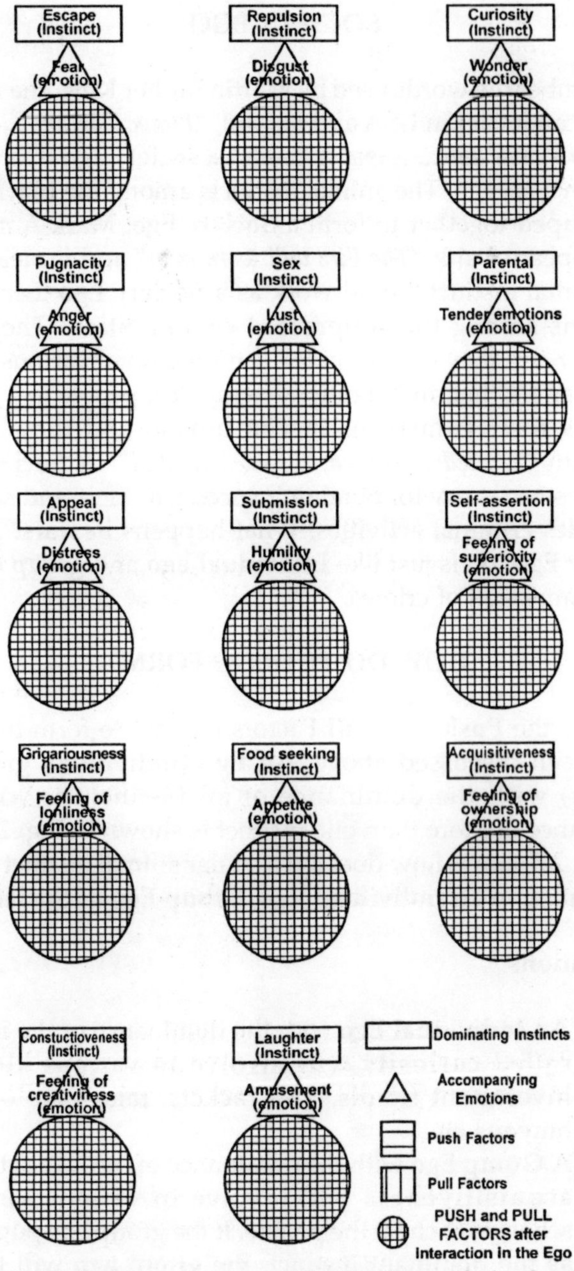

Fig. 2.5: Individual Ego, Group Ego, Society Ego with the dominance of an instinct with accompanying emotions.

3. A **Society Ego** with the dominance of the instinct **self-assertion** will have charity frauds, terrorist activities, communal fights, etc. to show their superiority.

There can be **egos** with the dominance of more than one animal instinct. Thus, there may be **egos** with **repulsion** and **pugnacity** as the dominant instincts. How is the dominance of the animal instincts reduced by **spirituality, morality/ethics** and **intelligence** is of paramount importance to reduce crimes in society. Actually the schools, character building institutions, family, religion, media, etc. make attempts to reduce crimes in society by inculcating moral/ethical, spiritual and intellectual inputs into the **ego** of individuals, groups and society. In order to do so, the **pull factors** may help a lot. This is the reason why we want to have value oriented education, god-fearing atmosphere at home, good media and publications, association with friends who have an upright conscience rightly formed etc. How do we develop an upright **ego** rightly formed?

FORMATION OF AN UPRIGHT CONSCIENCE (EGO) RIGHTLY FORMED: HOW IS IT?

Animal instincts are at work always as they are the activators of behaviour. They are needed for good behaviour as well as for bad behaviour. If it is for bad behaviour, then demonology spoke about demons working behind. Demons are said to have only evils in them and precisely therefore, the evils must be counter-attacked. For it, man should have goodness. In order to be good, people want to have God's help. In order to be good, the society created educational institutions, police and a legal system, moral preachers, value creators and so on. It is found necessary to have such character builders and value creators for the formation of an upright **ego** which is rightly formed. All those **EGO** formators are put under **pull factors.**

Illustrations

1. **Pull Factors** which are likely to form a defective **ego**

(conscience) are—(1) disorganized family, (2) broken family, (3) divorced family, (4) problem family, (5) obscene literature, (6) bad neighbourhood, (7) crime-causing media, (8) bad friendship, (9) crime-prone slum-life, (10) gang contact, (11) association with drug addicts, (12) police corruption, (13) corrupt society, (14) communalism (15) moral malpractices, (16) religious neglect, (17) unemployment and underemployment, (18) wrong political affiliations, (19) crime stimulating *'...isms'*, *'...ologies'* and *'...sophies'*, etc. and many more.

2. **Pull Factors** which are likely to form an upright **ego** in the right direction are—(1) value oriented education, (2) caring parents, (3) home and emotions, (4) fine schooling, (5) good teachers, (6) religious atmosphere, (7) moral upbringing, (8) good literature and publications, (9) fine motion pictures and TV serials (10) respecting parents, (11) good cultural activities, (12) best friendship, (13) good recreational facilities, (14) role models, (15) attractive *'...isms'*, *'...ologies'* and *'...sophies'*, (16) healthy food and nutrition, (17) harmonious co-existence, (18) dearth of fights and conflicts, (19) atmosphere promoting good human relations, and (20) crime-free social life and many more.

CAUSE-EFFECT RELATIONSHIP BETWEEN PULL FACTORS AND FORMATION OF AN UPRIGHT EGO (CONSCIENCE) RIGHTLY FORMED

There is no guarantee that the **pull factors**—positive in nature—will make an upright **Ego** rightly formed. For, the theory of causality—i.e., cause-effort relationship—is not applicable in **ego formation.** Nevertheless, there is a higher chance to make an upright **Ego** rightly formed in such situations. Likewise, negative **pull factors** need not necessarily create an **Ego** wrongly formed. Instances are there that daughters/girls born and brought up in brothels becoming girls with very high and positive sex-values. They do not opt for prostitution. Reversely enough, girls brought up in good atmosphere develop a *criminal ego*. The theory of causality is no more applicable while the theory of causation has some good relevance and applicability in the formation of an upright **ego** in individuals, groups and society.

No one on earth will be able to say the whole or total number of **pull factors** around an individual, group or society. People speak about prejudices and preconceived notions. For example, in India, people belonging to the higher castes have a lot of prejudices against the members of the lower castes. The reverse too may be true and such prejudices may affect their interpersonal (personnel) relations. Hence, the prejudices are considered to be **pull factors** affecting interpersonnel (personal) contacts. Within the group, there may be sub-groups and prejudices may work among the members of the different groups forming a society. This may be a **pull factor** and the individual, group or society **Ego** may be thus formed. In my view, it is just impossible to form an upright **Ego** which is rightly formed. Formation of an **upright ego rightly formed** may be a very good way to express an idea—nice to hear the phrase—but really very difficult to put it in practice. Therefore, everyone possess an **ego** which is likely to commit crimes at any time. The same is true in the case of a group or a society. For example, instances are plenty to show 'god-men' caught for criminal activities. They are brought up in an enviable atmosphere, so that, their **ego** will be developed in an upright way in the right direction. Likewise, a whole group or a society as a whole may commit crimes owing to the defective formation of an **ego** or owing to other factors. Hence, there is no Individual, Group or Society Ego which is uprightly formed in the right direction.

PUSH FACTORS OTHER THAN THE ANIMAL INSTINCTS

Let us take the **push factors**—say, **spirituality.** The **spirituality** is, as said earlier with **belief** or with **faith. Belief** in something as true may be seen in thousand and one matters. It may be seen in rationalism, empiricism, idealism, atheism, agnosticism, epicurianism, hedonism, sophism, existentialism, humanism, rationalism, demonology, theology, sociology etc. Likewise, the **Faith** may be with God and the God may be a personal God, Human God, *Avatars* (Incarnates of God), animals, snakes and so on. Which **belief** or **faith** will dominate the **ego** among the **push factors**? There are people who sacrifice children to please gods and belief in superstition may be seen in the **Ego.** Hindus may say something, Christians may say something else, Islam may say quite another thing and in such situations, how can an **Ego** be formed in an upright way in the right direction? Democracy, autocracy, socialism, communism, bureaucracy etc. have their own beliefs and how to form an upright **Ego** in the **Right** direction? Impossible.

What about the **Morality/Ethics?** The same position is seen there too. For some, there is absolute morality, for some others there is only relative morality. For some, morality is the lack of opportunities and for others morality is purely individualistic. For some, morality can be split and for others, morality cannot be split. For some, there is professional ethics and for others there is nothing called professional ethics. For them, morality and ethics are one and the same.

For some, divorce is an acceptable option and for others, it is not. Some favour mercy killing (euthanasia) and some do not. Some want abortion and some do not. Some say "victory *via* the barrel of the gun" while some are against it. For some, "end justifies the means", while for others, "the end and means must be justifiable". Some are in favour of terrorism while some are in favour of insurgency. Some are inclined to involve in organized crimes while some are not. Thus, we see people with different morality/ethics in society. All are moral/ethical and if one behaves against the morality/ethics, he feels or should feel "Guilty". Hence, the feeling of guilt when an act is committed or omitted is the measuring scale or criteria to decide whether or not one is moral or ethical in his outlook. One may see a **Group** to be moral or ethical as well as immoral or unethical. Likewise, a society as a whole may be moral/ethical or immoral/ unethical.

MORALITY/ETHICS AND SPIRITUALITY IN WATER-TIGHT COMPARTMENTS?

I do not subscribe to the view that the **spirituality** and **morality/ ethics** are in water-tight compartments. They are mixed together and make a whole in human mind. Again, the **animality (instincts)** is not in water-tight compartment. The instincts too are mixed with the **morality/ethics** and **spirituality.** This mixing is seen in **individual mind, in group mind** and in **society mind.**

Intelligence having memory, expansion, comprehension, critical analysis and intuitiveness plays its role with morality/ ethics, spirituality and animality. Everything has an intellectual back-up and therefore, one wants an intellectual analyis to make everything acceptable and justifiable. Thus, the **push factors** from a **whole** and in fact this **whole (push factors)** has interactions with the **pull factors.** It is shown in Fig. 2.6.

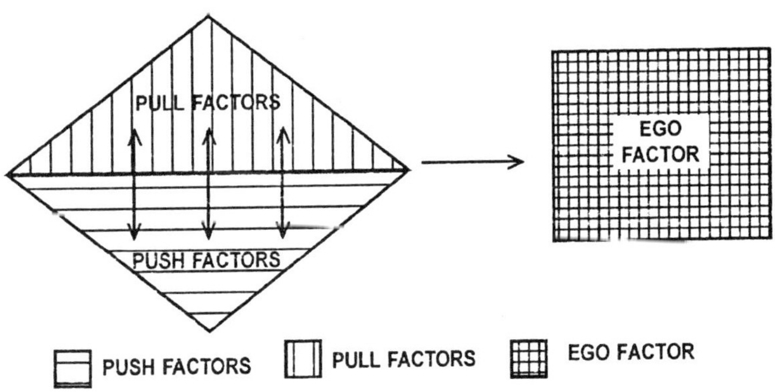

Fig. 2.6: Interaction between the PUSH FACTORS and PULL FACTORS to make an EGO FACTOR.

The **Ego Factor** thus formed may be:

(1) Individual Ego
(2) Group Ego
(3) Society Ego

Actually, it is this **Ego** which interacts with the **pull factors** as and when situations arise. The **ego** thus formed is dynamic and grows older and older as one grows older and experienced. As pointed out else where, some psychologists subscribe to the view that the **foundation** of the **ego** and **ego factor** in an individual are laid by the time he/she reaches the puberty. Afterwards, the age and experience have only superstucture constructed on the foundation. The **group ego** and the **society ego** are formed out of the **individual egos** forming the **group ego** and **society ego.** Thus, we may say that the **foundation** of the **ego** and **ego factor** of the **group ego** and **society ego** are constructed just like the **individual ego** and **ego factor** before they reach the puberty.

3
Animality: A Factor Activating Human Behaviour

No doubt, a man is a living animal. He eats, moves, procreates, excretes and dies—just like the animals do. In Charles Darwin's (1809-82) theory of evolution, man is evolved from apes and therefore, the specific difference (s.d.) of man from animality is his **rationality**—thus believed by scientists earlier. Man is a **rational animal**—this was the definition/description given by earlier philosophers. As science advanced further and psychology developed, the old definition is changed and a man is now defined or described as a **moral/ethical, intellectual, spiritual animal** which means that man has morality/ethics, intelligence, spirituality in him i.e., more than mere **rationality** as seen by earlier philosophers.

My research observations prove—

(1) All men are like all animals
(2) Some men are like some animals
(3) No man is like any other animals

All human beings are like all animal beings. Both man and animals, as said above eat, procreate, move, excrete, die etc. In that way, man behaves/can behave just like any other animals and they do so because of their instincts. Psychologists have identified instincts on the basis of their strength and power. It has been proved that maternal instinct is the most powerful instinct in man and animals. The instincts are expressed in very many ways. Animals express or exhibit them in their own way and human beings do so in their own way. All animals have got sense organs just like the man has them. They get stimulus and the sense organs receive them. On perception of the stimulus, man and animals behave more or less in the same way. Nevertheless, in certan situations, man cannot behave in the way animals behave and it is so because of the intervention of man's morality/ethics, spirituality, intelligence or more than one of them. More about this will be discussed later.

Some human beings are like some other animal beings. In weight, height etc., some people are like some animals. Man walks on two feet and some animals do so; some animals are vegetarians while some men are non-vegetarians. Some animals can drink water just like man and man cannot do it by licking as the dog does. Some animals can climb a tree just like some people do it. Some animals play with people while some others do not.

No human being is just like any other animal beings. Animals are not moral/ethical, spiritual or intellegent (of course, in certain animals, a grain of intelligence—e.g., memory may be seen). No animal is jealous just like the man is. We do not see complexes in animals as we notice in some people. Animals do not have personality or personality traits. I do not think that animals have imagination or intuitiveness. They do not have the capacity to make a critical analysis and thus the human kingdom is very much different from the animal kingdom.

I have no difficulty to accept the postulates of Charles Darwin (1809-82) as far as the evolution of man is concerned. No doubt, animality is the foundation of man and any human behaviour has its base or foundation in instincts. Animals behave out of their instinctual energy while man behaves out of his instincts, morality/ethics, spirituality and intelligence. This is called **drives** in man. The **drive** has its root in **instincts** of animals.

I have noticed all these instincts in animals in various forms. Nevertheless, I could not see the accompanying emotions in them. For example, I have seen constructiveness in insects, birds

Table 3.1: Instincts in Animals (McDougall)

Sl. No.	*Instincts*	*Accompanying Emotions*
1.	Escape	Fear
2.	Repulsion	Disgust
3.	Curiosity	Wonder
4.	Pugnacity (combat)	Anger
5.	Sex	Lust
6.	Parental	Tender emotions
7.	Appeal	Distress
8.	Submission	Humility
9.	Self-assertion	Feeling of superiority
10.	Gregariousness	Feeling of loneliness
11.	Food seeking	Appetite
12.	Acquisitiveness	Feeling of ownership
13.	Constructiveness	Feeling of creativeness
14.	Laughter	Amusement

and animals. But I have not seen the feeling of creativeness in them. Of course, I see it among the human beings. Before we discuss more, I want to direct you to the simple dictionary meanings [*Random House College Dictionary*] of all the instincts and emotions given above. They are given at the end of this chapter. I do not quote from a dictionary of psychology as I find many definitions/descriptions given by many psychologists on one and the same instinct are different.

How to draw the animal instincts?

Instincts

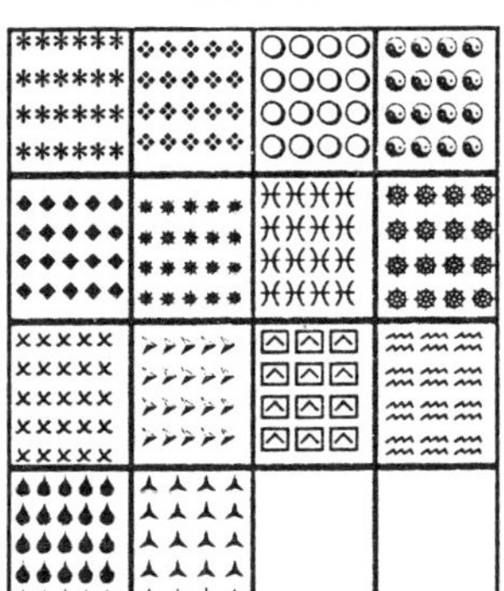

Fig. 3.1: 14 columns with different symbols represent-14 instincts identified so far. 2 columns are left blank to add more instincts if and when they are identified.

ACTIVATION BY ANIMAL INSTINCTS

The activating force in animals is **instincts** and in man, it is **drives** (Animality + Spirituality + Morality/Ethics + Intelligence together forming an **ego factor**). How do the **drives** activate man? It is as under:

1. Whenever a **stimulus** is perceived, the **ego factor** responds.
2. In the **ego factor,** one can see Animality, Morality/ Ethics, Spirituality and Intelligence. Out of these four contents of the **ego factor,** one of them overpowers the others. For example, a man feels hungry. The **instinct** of **Food Seeking** is activated and it overpowers the others with the result that he may involve in the commission of a crime to get the food if it is not legally obtainable. When a man has sex starvation, the instinct of **sex** overpowers the others with the result that he may commit rape or resort to masturbation if normal channels for sexual satisfaction is not available. Sigmund Freud said that an excessiveness or overeffect of the ID (instincts) will cause crimes. In my theory, the excessiveness and overeffect should be such that they must overpower the other contents in the **ego** to commit a crime.

EXCESSIVENESS OF INSTINCTS IN INDIVIDUALS, GROUP AND SOCIETY

Excessiveness or overeffect of **Animal Instincts** overpowering the other contents—say, **Spirituality, Morality/Ethics, Intelligence** of the **EGO** can and will cause crimes.

Illustration

A person suffers from a circular conflict owing to sexual starvation as seen in the Fig. 3.2.

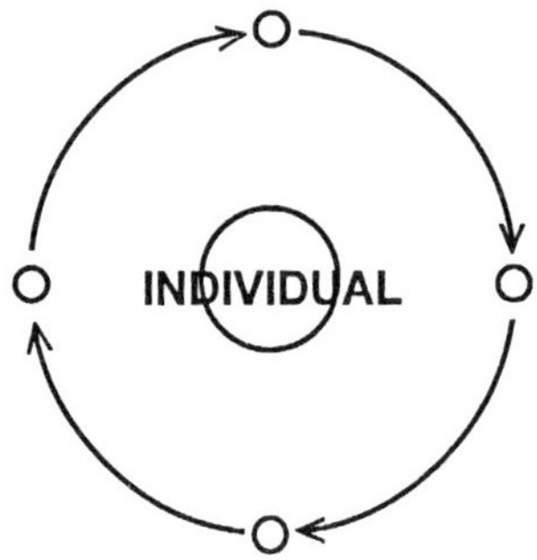

Fig. 3.2: Circular conflict in an individual.

He has mental conflicts and he cannot get out of them. From his **morality/ethics** mind: *"Is it morally right to have masturbation to get out of the circular conflict I have?"* His **morality/ethical** mind says: *"It is morally wrong to do so"*. Again, he experiences mental conflict. He asks his **Intelligence:** *"Is it harmful to health to have masturbation?"* The answer is: *"It is physically harmful to have masturbation."* Again, he experiences mental conflict and he asks his **Spirituality**: *"Is it a sin spiritually to masturbate?"* and the answer is: *"It is"*. Then what to do? The animal instinct of Sex is very powerful and is excessive. It, therefore, has an overeffect and overpowers the **Spirituality, Morality/Ethics and Intelligence.** He masturbates and gets relieved of his sexual frustration/conflict.

It may be noted that one out of the 14 instincts overpowers at a given time and in some cases, there may be two or more, nevertheless only one of the instincts may have the dominance over the others.

Illustration

A man is harassed by another or is victimized. He decides to react and his **pugnacity** (combat) comes as the instinct to manage the situation. Though **pugnacity** (combat) is the dominant instinct activating at that moment, **self-assertion, escape** and **repulsion** (3 instincts) may also support or co-operate with the dominant instinct called **pugnacity** (combat). He murders the one harassing or victimising him.

There are situations in which his **Morality/Ethics, Spirituality or Intelligence** overpowering the **animality** in which case he may not commit a crime. In certain cases, **Morality/Ethics** alone or along with others may have the dominant effect while in other situations, his **spirituality** alone or along with others may have the dominance. In both cases, he may not commit the murder.

A group may have animal instincts. Once, a policeman was beaten on the road by a group of people. The policemen in group came out and started physically attacking the people expressing **pugnacity** (Combat). The group consisting of policemen had **pugnacity** (Dominant Animal Instinct) supported by **self-assertion.** A Commission of Inquiry was appointed and the Commission found fault with the policemen. According to them, the policemen as a group ought to have behaved from their **moral/ethical** mind and not from the **Animal Mind.** The group, thus, may have a group mind.

There were two student associations formed on the basis of political affiliations. One group has **Repulsion** against the other and precisely therefore each group indulged in several criminal activities against the rival group. During the college elections, one group exhibitted many posters showing repulsion which ultimately culminated in mutual fights, stone throwings and police interventions.

What about the society? A society consists of sub-societies. India has many castes/sub-castes. There are many religions. I have seen that the animal instincts found operative in a society cause great havoc on other society/sub-society. The communal riots, religious bigotry, racial conflicts, political fights, agrarian unrest etc. are examples in point. Simple things become big. A spark may turn into a wild fire and murders and mass scale destruction may be resulted. In many freedom struggles, one may see such animal instincts powerfully operating causing many types of crimes. What happens in wars? Nations against nations, religion against other religions, denominations against other denominations, sects against other sects, labourers against the management, political parties against other political parties, terrorists against a whole society, fundamentalists against fanatics and thus we may find animal instinct of one society functioning or reacting against another society. Thus, the history of the world is the history of instinctual behaviour expressed in this way or that way. As far as the criminal behaviour is concerned, there is the fight between the haves and have nots, between the weaker sections against the strong, between the handicapped against the powerful. In all crimes, therefore, one observes the uncontrolled instinctual forces at the root of the act/omission—no matter, the crime is committed by individuals, groups, or societies.

CRIMINALITY AND INSTINCTS

All instincts are necessary and needed for activating animals or man as the case may be. All beyond a limit become criminal in nature as shown in the Fig. 3.3.

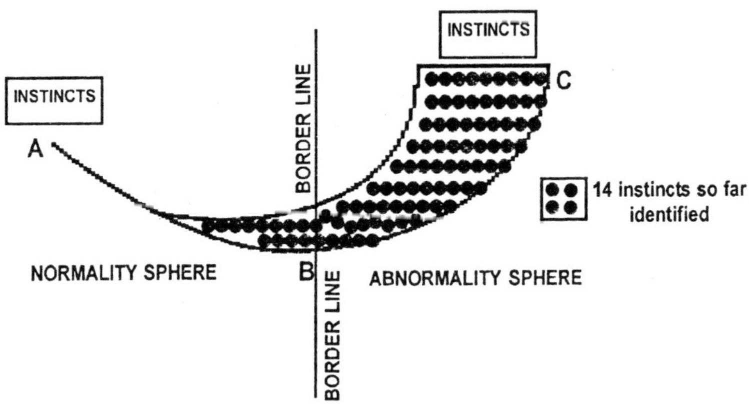

Fig. 3.3: Normality, Abnormality Curve.

What is a normal instinct? i.e., non-criminal in nature? It is just a common characteristic to have **curiosity** when one sees a special or peculiar thing. This is normal and it is applicable to all 14 instincts. A mother sees her child after a few years and it is just natural to have the parental instincts coming up with accompanying tender emotions. Anyone in her place will express such an instinct.

The curve (Fig. 3.3) shows the instincts of a person moving from an absolute **normality (A)** to an absolute **criminality (C).** When the instinct is at **A,** his behaviour is perfect, quite normal and necessary as an activating force. When it moves from **A** to **B,** he is gradually behaving more and more criminal (abnormal) and when he crosses **B,** he is crossing the threshold of normality of instinctual behaviour i.e., normality sphere and enters into the criminal (abnormality) sphere. As one's behaviour is still moving forward in the criminality sphere—without the influence of **morality/ethics, spirituality** and **intelligence,** he will be committing crimes or criminal (abnormal) behaviour. Anybody can become criminal at any time if his **morality/ethics, spirituality and intelligence** spheres are dormant or inactive or inoperative. Any instinct can/will cross the threshold if and when the **morality/ethics, spirituality or intelligence** are dormant, inactive or inoperative.

ANIMALITY AND CRIMINAL LIABILITY

Animals have no criminal liability. For, an animal does not know what it is doing. In order to establish the criminal liability, one should know the nature of the act/omission, the consequence of the act/omission or what he/she is doing is contrary to the law in force. Animals do not have such an awareness and therefore, there is no legal or criminal liability for animals. I think that there was only one occasion in legal history that a pig was hanged in the west to have caused the death of a human being. In law, killing of a human being by another human being is considered to be a culpable homicide. Animals behave from their **animality** which consists of only instincts. In the **animal kingdom,** one sees the survival of the fittest and one animal is killed by another, at times, for food. Lions, cheetah and such other carnivores animals do so and the same is seen among the birds, insects, reptiles and fishes. Birds can commit theft of fruits, grains and the fishes can trespass into any territory. Spiders eat flies. Perhaps, animals, birds, insects and fishes commit all sorts of offences defined by man in the penal laws, moral laws, social laws, cultural laws, ethical laws etc. However, man cannot do so. For, he is punished if he commits an act/omits to perform an act which is defined as crime by any law. Why? The human behaviour is judged by a **morality/ethics** scale and some times by a **spirituality** scale or by an **intelligence** scale or by two or more of them.

MORALITY/ETHICS, SPIRITUALITY AND INTELLIGENCE SCALES

As repeatedly said, the activating force in any human behaviour is the animal instinct called **drive** in men. No doubt, a man is an animal and is a moral/ethical, spiritual and intellectual **being** activated by **animal instincts.** Precisely therefore, the morality/ethics, spirituality and intelligence scales are utilized to assess, evaluate and judge the behaviour of man to be human or otherwise—in other words, the behaviour is criminal or otherwise. Man cannot and should not behave from **instincts.** Remember always that all human made laws have a **moral base** or **moral foundation.** All God-made (Divine?) Laws have a **spiritual base or foundation.** Most of the so named Divine Laws (Religious laws) have a **moral base** or **foundation.** For, laws without a moral base/foundation are no laws at all. Again all laws—moral or otherwise—have or should have an intellectual explanation, interpretation, rationalization or justification as the case may be.

Illustrations

1. A man kills another. The foundation may be any one or more of the 14 animal instincts.

Moral Scale: Is the killing justified/justifiable. The killing was for private defence. Hence, it is a justifiable homicide.

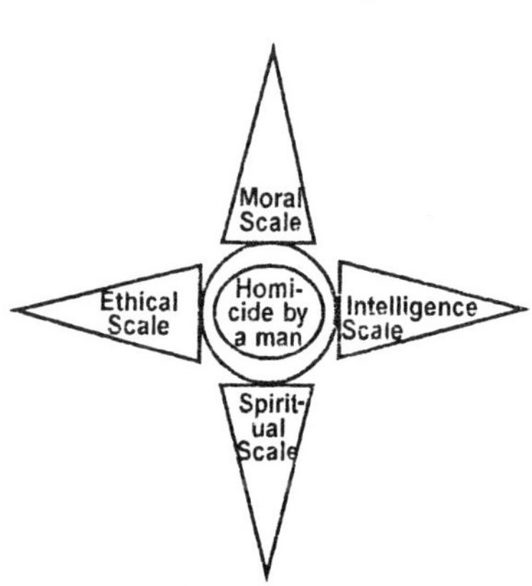

Fig. 3.4: Scales to decide criminality.

Ethical Scale: Is the killing excusable? The killing was done while law and order management necessitated it. Hence, it is excusable.

Spiritual Scale: The killing was done when no other option was available. Hence, the killing is religiously acceptable. In *Mahabharata Yuddha* in *Bhagavad Gita*, mass killings were approved as the performance of *Dharma* and hence, religiously accepted.

Intellectual Scale: On a critical analysis of all the **Pull factors,** the killing was necessitated by the environments. Hence, there is no criminal liability for the homicide.

One may take any law—social, religious, moral, ethical, penal, cultural and evaluate the human act/omission by the help of the scales given above to fix the criminal liability for the same.

HOW FAR ONE MAY GO WITHOUT VIOLATING THE LAW?

I may say that one can go up to the threshold of criminality without violating the law. If he proceeds further from the threshold of criminality, the crime becomes serious or henious. In Christianity, they speak about venial sins and mortal sins, in Indian penal laws, they say cognizable and non-cognizable offences, in the west, they speak about felony and misdemeanor. In all sorts of crimes committed, animal instinct is the root cause.

INDIVIDUAL ANIMALITY, GROUP ANIMALITY AND SOCIETY ANIMALITY

We have seen that all individuals have **Animality** (instincts) in them. The question is: Is there **Animality** (Instincts) in **groups?** My studies show that the **groups** have **group instincts.** HOW?

Illustrations

In my case diary, I may show any number of instances in which the groups have behaved instinctively. What happens in a situation of mob violence? In mob violence, people take law in their hands and the reason, morality/ethics, intelligence etc., have no scope there.

In traffic accident cases, people behave instinctively. Road rage is notorious and instances are plenty to show that the drivers were beaten and, in some instances, to death. When a woman is molested by a man in public, the group turns violent expressing animality there. Moral policing in Kerala is assessed to be the expression of the animal mind by a group. When a pick pocket is caught, there will be group violence on him.

What is seen in aggressive crowd is the expression of animality. It is an aggressive crowd which is an unorganized throng willing to be led into lawlessness. Panicky crowd which takes law in their hands behaves from animality. The acquisitive crowd—e.g., food riots and lootings—may become a mob expressing animality. When a **group animality** is examined by an investigation team or by a Commission of Inquiry, then the **morality/ethics, spirituality** or **intelligence** scales may be applied to fix the criminal liability.

What about the **group animality** of organized groups like criminal gangs, dacoits, army, police, religious or communal congregations etc.? They too behave, some times, instinctively. They may use their muscle-power and money power to violate the laws. An examination or scrutiny of their behaviour may show that the application of mind power was lacking in their behaviour. Mind Power means **morality/ethics, spirituality** and **intelligence.**

As far as **society-animality** is concerned, I have got enough real incidents of communal riots and religious bigotry in some situations. They plan in advance to behave from their instinctual area and thereby to cause chaos and confusion in society leading to serious law and order problems causing mass murders. I do not want to enumerate such **society-animality** expressing situations in any country. Nevertheless, one may see law and order violations between—(1) religion and religion, (2) one sect in a religion against another sect in the same religion, (3) communal riots, (4) political agitations causing serious damages to property, (5) one political party against another political party, (6) one sect in a political party against another in the same party, (7) political party *vs.* communal parties, (8) agrarian unrest, (9) student agitations, (10) refugee problems, (11) labour strikes, and (12) agitations by the suppressed community or oppressed sections of the society and thus one sces animality expressed in committing a series of public order crimes in society. Sometimes, police officers behave from their animality and they do so as individuals, as a group and even as a society.

It has been observed that morality/ethics, spirituality and intelligence can be applied or insisted on groups/society etc., only by leaders or by the hierarchy. The leaders in politics, religion, community and society apply the moral, ethical, intellectual and spiritual principles to control the people when they behave from their instinctual sphere.

DIFFERENCE BETWEEN MAN AND ANIMAL IN EXPRESSING ANIMALITY

Both man and animals are **animals** and the man is an **animal** with a difference. Animals behave instinctively while man behaves instinctively being supported by morality/ethics, spirituality and intelligence. Now, there are countries which accept unisex marriages. Sociologists give special and specific definition for **"marriage"** and precisely therefore some of them do not accept "unisex living together" to be called marriage. According to them "unisex living together" is only an instinctual expression to satisfy only the lust. But the advocates of "unisex marriages" give moral sanctity to such animal behaviour. As a result, there is the legal sanction for the lust enjoyment. What about the spirituality? Though the religious men and theologians may speak against such living together, there is a section of atheists accepting such unisex marriages as desirable. Intellectual analysis too does not disfavour it and therefore man justifies that animal behaviour to be a normal behaviour—non-criminal in nature. Criminology accepts the fact that the concept of crime and criminal behaviour is dynamic so much so that the crime today may not be a crime tomorrow or rather a virtue, day after tomorrow. Hence, the **Push-Pull-Ego Factor Theory** of crime causation is an approach to understand crime and criminal behaviour today—*hic et nunc.* There is no eternal theory in social sciences and precisely therefore, I claim that my **Push-Pull-Ego Factor Theory** of crime is an approach to understand the causation-factors in crime and criminal behaviour.

MAN IS NOT AN ANIMAL, BUT MANY ANIMALS...

Man is a rational animal—and that is what philosophers said long ago. I had an opportunity to study Philosophical Psychology and then I studied about the animality in man as the philosophers saw it. At a time philosophical psychology was in vogue, instincts or animal instincts were not well known to the then scholastic philosophers.[1] Anyway, when they were asked to say about the **animal** in man, they did not or could not name the special or specific animal in man. Is it the elephant?—the lion?—the giraffe?—the goat?—the dog?—the monkey?-the chimpanzee? or all of them? As a criminologist interested in studying crime and criminal behaviour, I noticed that man is not a **Rational Animal,** but he is "**Many Animals**" or "**All animals**". Sometimes, man behaves more animal like than the animals themselves. Animals are not jealous, not vindictive, do not have any complexes, do not have personality, not trained they do not imitate, not suggestive, do not identify, are not emotional etc., but the man is. Man behaves instinctively with a vengeance, with retribution, with vindictiveness, with jealousy, with cruelty, with negativism etc. Hence, in my view, a man is not only many animals, but also many animals with at times diabolic emotions, attitudes and approaches. He makes use of his intelligence to execute his instincts diabolically. No animal kills an animal with 51 or 61 stabbings whereas a man does so. No animal attacks another animal with jealousy or vindictiveness whereas a man does. No doubt man should have **morality/ethics, spirituality** and **intelligence** to desist from committing crimes and showing criminal behaviour. Even countries attack other countries and behave with multi-animal instincts without any cause or justifications. What happens in wars, in bombing and mass killings? Grenade crimes are committed by individuals and innocents are killed. What do the terrorists do? What do the insurgents do? They kill the innocents for parochial interests whereas animals attack other animals for feeding or to escape from dangers. But man? In my view, man is not a rational animal, but is "many birds, fishes, reptiles, insects and animals" put together.

ANIMALITY AND PUNISHMENT TO CRIMES

It has been observed by me that no instincts in animals, birds, fishes, insects and reptiles can be eradicated or stopped by way of punishment. For example, we can make an animal starve by denying food, but the moment the animal is provided with food, then it will start eating it whatever may be the punishment given to it. Likewise, any crime committed by man out of instincts can never be prevented or stopped by means of punishment. By constant and continuous inculcation of moral, ethical, spiritual or intellectual values, the instincts in man can be channelized and to that extent, the crime/criminal behaviour is reduced. Reduction of crimes is as said by me earlier, quite possible, but prevention or total eradication of crime is impossible. Hence, the conclusions arrived by me through researches are—

(1) Crimes committed by animal instincts can never be totally eliminated, prevented, or eradicated. The instinctual energy can be channelized to other areas by inculcation of moral, ethical, intellectual or spiritual values.

(2) Crimes committed by animal instincts can never be fully prevented or permanently stopped by

punishment, however severe it may be. The instinctual energy can be converted to another energy and thus a particular crime reduction is possible.

(3) There exists a quota of instinctual crimes and the quota is necessary for the existence and survival and development of the society. Crimes above the quota needed for a society can only be reduced.

(4) One category of instinctual crimes may be converted to another category of instinctual crimes just like one type of energy is converted to another type of energy.

What should be the type of punishment for instinctual crimes is a topic of discussion even today and the punishment is awarded by trial and error methods. Will a retributive approach be effective to curb down instinctual crimes? Will a deterrent punishment reduce instinctual crimes? Will correction, reformation, rehabilitation and reintegration to society by way of incarceration be of any use for the reduction or prevention of instinctual crimes? Criminologists and Penologists are conducting researches to study the effect of punishments on instinctual criminals now.

MORALITY/ETHICS, SPIRITUALITY AND INTELLIGENCE OVER ANIMALITY (INSTINCTS)

If we study Fig. 3.5, we will notice that the **morality/ethics, spirituality** and **intelligence** are developed in an upright way in the right direction to form the **ego factor.**

Why should the **moral/ethical mind, spiritual mind** and **intellectual mind** be developed in an upright way in the right direction by the **pull factors**? They are necessary for controlling the Animality in man. As said elsewhere, the root cause of all criminal acts are seen in the **instincts** and the instincts can be controlled only by developing the **moral/ ethical, intellectual** and **spiritual minds** in an upright way in the right direction.

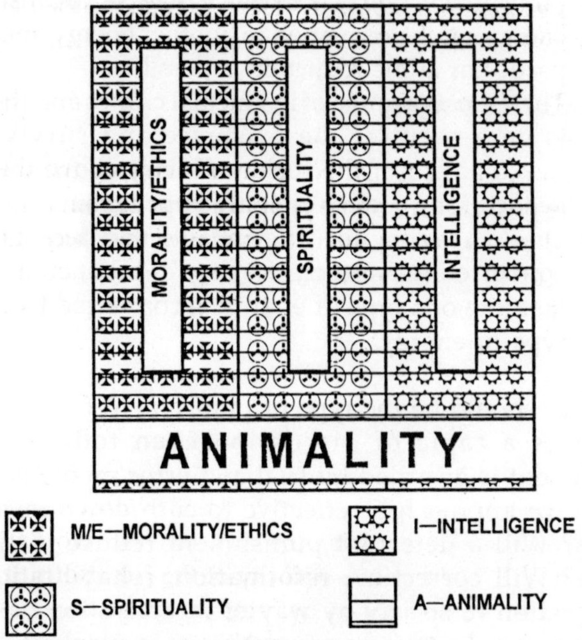

Fig. 3.5: The base is A and the M/E, S&I are seen—not in watertight compartments but mixed together just like pure water mixed with salt water, sugar water and bitter water.

How do you decide the uprightness and right direction? For this, there exist some criteria or scales and they are—

1. ***Subjective Scale***
2. ***Normative Scale***
3. ***Socio-cultural Scale***
4. ***Statistical (Majority) Scale***
5. ***Clinical Scale.***

They are discussed as follows:

1. Subjective Scale

This is also called **'Individualistic Scale'**. Owing to the interaction with the **pull factors,** some take to themselves a principle: ***"honesty is the best policy"*** or ***"commission of a***

crime is an unpardonable act." Here, they shape their **ego factor** accordingly and thus the 'instincts' are controlled.

2. Normative Scale

This is also called **'ideal scale'** and owing to the interaction with the **pull factors**, some people accept certain principles as the ideal principles for them. Sometimes, they accept the great sayings of the great men as the ideal. For example: ***"Don't commit a crime, because it is a sin against humanity".*** Accordingly, they control their animal instincts.

3. Statistical Scale

This is also called **majority** Scale. In Malayalam language, there is a saying: ***"If three people out of four do an act in a particular way, do it as the majority does it".*** In other words, majority of the people are right in majority of the situations. It follows, therefore, that the animal instincts are to be controlled—and everyone must not allow any instinct to cross the permitted or permissible limits. There are people who practise "mortification, fasting, self-penance" etc. for the purpose of controlling their animal instincts. In fact, my parents forced me to have recourse to motifications just to develop an instinctual control over my behaviour.

4. Socio-cultural Scale

The society imposes certain **"Do's and Don'ts"** to effect control over the animal instincts found operating among the people. **"Don't urinate in public"** is a social norm imposed. Again, the culture imposes certain "norms" to control animal instincts in people. Such controls are there in actions and words spoken. How to behave in society is taught by the culture and thus the animal instincts are controlled by the culture prevailing in any society.

5. Clinical Scale

This is also called **'Diagnostic Scale'** and accordingly, man is asked to evaluate his behaviour from two angles, namely, from: (1) the individual angle, (2) the social angle. If the expression of an animal instinct gives individual pleasure as well as ensures social welfare, then there is no harm in accepting such a behavioural pattern. On the other hand, if the behaviour gives only individual pleasure and not social welfare, then avoid such behaviour whatever may be the intensity or strength of the animal instinct. Again, if the behaviour ensures social welfare, but no individual satisfaction, then avoid such behaviour too however strong may be the instinctual pressure.

Now, there are moralists and theologians who think that the clinical scale ought to take into account the individual dimension, the social dimension, the moral dimension and the divine dimension when they control the animal instincts. In law, all crimes are treated as crimes against the society-against humanity. This is the reason why crimes are investigated by the police, prosecuted by the Government prosecutors and the guilty are punished. The incarcerated are housed in the Centres of Personality Development (Prisons) for their correction. The people (tax-payers) or the society invests a lot of money for their reintegration back to society. The society hates crimes and not the crime-doers or criminals.

Notes

1. Scholasticism, i.e., the system of theological and philosophical teachings predominant in the Middle Ages, based chiefly upon the authority of the church fathers and of Aristotle and his commentators.
2. The dictionary (Webster's) meanings of instincts and emotions are as under—

   Instincts

   1. **Escape**: (i) To slip or get away as from confinement or restraint; and (ii) avoid punishment or any threatened evil.
   2. **Repulsion**: (i) The act of repelling or driving back; and (ii) distaste, repugnance or aversion.

3. **Curiosity**: (i) A desire to learn or know about anything; and (ii) Inquisitiveness.
4. **Pugnacity (Combat)**: (i) Excessively inclined to quarrel or fight; and (ii) quarrelsome.
5. **Sex**: (i) The instinct or attraction drawing one sex toward another or its manifestation in life and conduct; and (ii) either the male or female division of a species especially. as differentiated with reference to the reproductive functions.
6. **Parental**: Of, pertaining to, or characteristic of a parent, i.e., father or mother.
7. **Appeal**: (i) An earnest request for aid, mercy etc.; and (ii) evoking or attracting interest.
8. **Submission**: (i) To yield to or to give over to the power or authority of another (often used reflexively); and (ii) Subject to some kind of treatment or influence.
9. **Self-Assertion**: (i) Stating with assurance, confidence or force by self; (ii) affirm by self; (iii) to maintain or defend (claims, rights etc.); and (iv) to put (one self) forward boldly and insistently.
10. **Gregariousness**: (i) Fond of the company of others; (ii) sociable; and (iii) living in flocks or herds as animals.
11. **Food-seeking**: (i) To go in search or quest of food; and (ii) try to find or discover by searching of food.
12. **Acquisitiveness**: (i) Tending or seeking to acquire and own, often greedily, (ii) come into possession of, (iii) get as one's own, and (iv) to gain for oneself through one's actions or efforts.
13. **Constructiveness**: (i) Helping to improve (opposed to destructiveness).
14. **Laughter**: (i) to express emotion, as mirth, pleasure derision or nervousness with an audible, vocal expulsion of air from the lung that can range from a loud burst of sound to series of quiet chuckles; and (ii) to experience mirth or derision.

Accopanying Emotions

1. **Fear** is the accompanying emotion of **escape** and it means accompanying **instincts** a (i) distressing emotion aroused by an impending pain, danger, evil etc., or by an illusion of such, (ii) anxiety, (iii) reverential owe especially toward God, and (iv) something of which one is afraid or that causes fright or apprehension. In Psychology, it may be real or unreal fear (phobia).
2. **Disgust** is the accompanying emotion of **Repulsion** and it means (i) to cause nausea or loathing in; and (ii) to offend the good taste, moral sense etc.
3. **Wonder** is the accompanying emotion of **Curiosity** and it means (i) to think or speculate curiously; (ii) to be filled with

admiration, amazement or owe; and (iii) the emotion excited by what is strange, admirable or surprising.

4. **Anger** is the accompanying emotion of **Pugnacity** and it means a strong feeling of displeasure and belligerence are used by a real or supposed wrong.
5. **Lust** is the accompanying emotion of **Sex** and it means (i) sexual, i.e., desire or appetite, esp. when uncontrolled or illicit; and (ii) a passionate or overmastering desire.
6. **Tender Emotions** is the accompanying emotions of **Parental** and it means (i) soft or delicate in substance; (ii) not hard or tough; and (iii) gentle, kind compassionate, affectionate, loving etc.
7. **Distress** is the emotion accompanying **Appeal** and it means (i) a cute physical or mental suffering, pain, anxiety or sorrow; and (ii) anything that causes pain, trouble or sorrow.
8. **Humility** is the emotion accompanying **Submission** and it means (i) the quality or the condition of being humble, modest, sense of one's own importance, rank, etc.
9. **Feeling of Superiority** is the accompanying emotion of **Self Assertion** and it means (i) higher in rank, station, degree, status etc.; (ii) above the average in excellence, merit, intelligence etc.; and (iii) of higher grade or quality.
10. **Feeling of Loneliness** is the emotion accompanying **Gregariousness** and it means (i) feeling lone, (ii) solitude, (iii) without company, (iv) companionless, and (v) destitute of friendly companionship or relationships.
11. **Appetite** is the emotion accompanying **Food Seeking** and it means (i) a desire for food or drink; (ii) any bodily need or craving; and (iii) a desire, fondness or inclination for food.
12. **Feeling of Ownership** is the emotion following **Acquisitiveness** and it means (i) of, pertaining to, or belonging to oneself or itself, and (ii) come into one's own.
13. **Feeling of Creativeness** is the emotion accompanying **Constructiveness** and it means to cause to come into being as something unique that would not naturally evolve or that is not made by ordinary processes.
14. **Amusement** is the emotion following **Laughter** and it means (i) to hold the attention of (some one) agreeably; (ii) entertain or divert in a pleasant manner; and (iii) to excite mirth or the like.

4
Intelligence: A Factor Distinguishing Human Behaviour

I may admit that a man is a rational[1] animal. Nevertheless, I may emphatically assert that he/she is not rational alone. He has memories and some of the memories never die. Trees have leaves and as days go on, leaves fall down. The fallen leaves may fly whenever there is a strong wind, nevertheless a few leaves will remain under the tree or in the near vicinity. Likewise, people may store only a few memories in their mind as many may be forgotten. It has been found that an intelligent person will have good memories of what he sensed. He does not forget. In Intelligence Tests conducted to measure I.Q., the memory is tested. When Sigmund Freud spoke about **conscious mind, sub-conscious mind and unconscious mind,** he said that the memories were stored in the **sub-conscious mind** of the man. Live and vivid matters were, according to him, in the **conscious mind.** He said that the more one could memorize, the more intelligent he would be.

In Malayalam language, there is a proverb: *"A cat fallen in hot water will be afraid of even cold water"* signifying that the memories work in animals too in a small way. Psychologists argue that the animals can be trained by conditioning and the taught matter remain in their 'memory', if it can be called so, in a small way. But in man, memory works well and he remembers many things when he behaves. *"Experience is the best teacher"*—is again a proverb and man resorts to booting in his memory. Some of the examinations in schools/colleges are intended to evaluate the memory and the quiz programmes in T.V. reality shows are intended in a way to measure the memory of the contestants. People learn a lot and keep them in their memory. There are Ayurvedic preparations in India to enhance the memory power and there are many techniques and methods to improve the memory power. During old age, it is seen that there occurs memory loss and Alzheimer's disease is a problem for the aged. Medical men and psychologists say then that the intelligence is impaired owing to memory loss and to that extent, his/her intellectual power is lost. So to say, in a nutshell **memory** is a function or power of intelligence. Rationality does not contain memory whereas intelligence does have. Hence, man is an intelligent animal meaning thereby that he can memorize things.

Like **memory,** man has the capacity to comprehend. The power of comprehension[2] is expressed in many ways. It is proved by researches that the more one is able to comprehend ideas, the more intelligent he is. During our High School (Secondary School studies), one sees **precis writing** in question papers. Three or four paragraphs are given in a lengthy way and the examined is asked to comprehend the ideas and express them in a paragraph reducing the length to 1/3rd of the original in the question paper. The one who has a good vocabulary, better understanding and clear thought processes, he comprehends the entire text and puts it down reducing the entire matter to its one third size within the time schedule. Whenever a person is asked to narrate the story of a three hours' lengthy film seen by him recently, one does it within five minutes, another may do it within 10 minutes and a third one may do it within 30 minutes depending upon each one's comprehending capacity and ability to express the idea in an understandable manner. The one who does it quickly is considered to be more intelligent while the others who do it slowly are treated to be less intelligent. Admitting that a man is rational, it does not mean that he has got the quick grasping capacity and ability to comprehend the ideas in a quick manner. Capacity for **'comprehension'** is the power of intelligence and precisely therefore man is an intelligent animal.

What is "**expansion?**"[3] During examinations or in extempore speeches, an idea is given and the candidates are asked to expand the concept or idea. For example, *"Obedience is better than sacrifice", "Mother and Goodness—are one and the same", "God is love", "Pride goes before every fall"* etc. are expanded to four or five pages by an intelligent person whereas a dull individual cannot do so. Some candidates speak for hours during extempore speeches and thus, the power of "**expansion**" is considered to be a parameter to measure the intelligence. While a man is a rational animal, it does not mean that he has the capacity for expanding the idea/concept to any length. Hence, man is an intelligent animal.

Critical analyis is an intellectual capacity and the one who makes such an analysis is found to be more intelligent than the one who does not. For making an analysis, logical thinking is necessary and one can resort to inductive logic or deductive logic, syllogisms, reasonings, rational interpretations, clear cut understanding, constructive criticisms, positive and negative thinkings, neutral approaches, arguments—*pro* and *contra,* philosophical outlooks, wide readings, scientific knowledge, experience and what not? Rationality does not mean all of those enumerated above and therefore man is an intelligent animal.

Intuitiveness[4] **Inventiveness, Imagination** etc. are other characteristics of intelligence. Philosophers, scientists, researchers and so on have higher I.Q. and precisely therefore they invent many things which ordinary people cannot. Issac Newton (1642-1727), Albert Einstein (1879-1955), Jesus Christ, Sri Sankara, Jean Paul Sartre (1905-1980) and so on had very high I.Q. and therefore they were called super intelligent. One hundred (100) I.Q. is enough for an ordinary person. People who are having below 100 I.Q. is considered to be retarded as they have a low I.Q. There are four subtypes, reflecting the degree of intellectual impairment and designated as Mild (50-70 I.Q.), Moderate (35-49 I.Q.), severe (20-34 I.Q.), and profound (below 20 I.Q.). Here, people having intuitiveness, inventiveness, imagination etc. are considered to be highly intelligent. Hence, man is an intelligent animal. There are many derivatives for the power of intelligence and they may be asthetics, persistence, sociability etc. of human beings.

During 1948, Psychologists found it convenient to identify three varieties of mental functions, namely—

(1) Mechanical intelligence, i.e., the ability to deal with things.
(2) Social intelligence, i.e., the ability to deal with people.
(3) Conceptual intelligence, i.e., the ability to deal with ideas and symbols.

Though this scheme of classification came into existence only around 1950, there were psychologists who developed the same or similar ideas even during 1920 and Jhorndike was the scientist who then classified intelligent activities into three types, viz., *social intelligence, concrete intelligence* and *abstract intelligence.*

INTELLIGENCE AND HUMAN BEHAVIOUR

Man is intelligent and precisely therefore, the animality in him (instincts) must be guided or controlled by **intelligence.** Goddard said long ago that low grade intelligence was the cause of crimes. During First World War, Intelligence Tests were designed to measure the I.Q. levels of the soldiers to fight intelligently in the war and thereby to ensure defeat of the enemies. Afterwards, the Intelligence Tests were administered to the convicts in prisons to ascertain whether or not they were mentally deficient or retarded inmates. To the great surprise, the researchers found that the prison population was as intelligent as the population outside. Thus, Goddard's theory was shattered into pieces.

At the same time, researches were conducted to learn the relationship between low I.Q. level, and criminality. Did the morons, imbeciles and idiots commit crimes which required high planning and execution? It was found out that they could not commit such crimes which required high intellectual calibre. They did or could commit only instinctual crimes like rapes, sexual attacks causing hurt, quarelling, committing theft of food items to satiate their hunger etc. There was a Malayalam film in which a moron was beaten for committing theft of an edible sweet from the shelves of a way-side tea shop. It showed the public attitude towards the mentally or intellectually deficient crime-doers.

The crime-doers who suffer from low I.Q. cannot distinguish between good or bad just like the animals. In the mental hospitals where the mentally retarded patients are housed, one may take note of naked people who do not know that they are naked. How can such people commit crimes which require high planning and execution? They are not seen anywhere in the vicinity of crime syndicates, international racketeering, *Mafia* operations, nexus criminality, bureaucratic and corporate crimes. From the discussion, it may be seen that intelligence will never become a **push** or **pull factor** in the causation of planned and well executed crimes. Intelligence may or will decide as to how intelligently a crime is executed, how intelligently the police is fooled and how intelligently an order of conviction is not passed by a court of law. Hence, it is argued that the causative force or energy to commit a crime should be located outside the intelligence.

ROLE OF INTELLIGENCE AND COMMISSION OF CRIMES

My researches taught me: "Criminals in general are not feeble minded people. The mentally retarded cannot involve themselves in organized crimes, crime-syndicates or white collar crimes or crimes requiring intelligence and planning"—thus I wrote in my book **Crime, Police and Correction** in 1998. I wrote further: *"People in general do not show any sympathy or consideration towards a person who is mentally retarded when he is caught for an instinctual crime he has committed. He is beaten and beaten severely. After all, he is mentally retarded and he deserves more sympathy and consideration than a person of intelligence."*

The crimes of intelligence are—

1. *White Collar Crimes:* Crimes committed by people having very high socio-economic status during the course of their profession for financial profit (see, E.H. Sutherland).
2. *Organized Crimes* including crime syndicates, racketeering etc. and it is committed by high planning and preparation with a lot of legal immunity and support from law enforcement officials and high ranking politicians (see, Oyster Bay Definition).
3. *Nexus Crimes*: Crimes committed by unholy nexus, among the bureaucrats, politicians and criminals, for financial profit and exhorbitant economic benefit (see, Dr. James Vadackumchery).
4. *JEL Crimes*: Crimes committed by the members of Judiciary, Executive and Legistalure *via* an unholy nexus (see, Dr. James Vadackumchery).
5. *Consensus Crimes*: Crimes committed by people after making an agreement.
6. *Bureaucratic Crimes*: Crimes committed by the bureaucrats for their manifold benefits *via* nefarious means and methods.
7. *Enforcement Crimes*: Crimes committed by law enforcement officials for their benefits and profits during the course of their work.
8. *Mafia and crimes of similar nature etc.:* Crimes committed by a group for their mutual benefits, especially financial.

Why do we call them **"Crime of Intelligence"**? They are called so, because—

1. They have good planning, execution and organization. The general public do not and cannot see the inner sides of the organization or planning etc.
2. Those who commit such crimes can give an intelligent explanation, rationalization, interpretation and

justification. They are able to convince people that they are doing a good thing.

3. The crimes are executed in most of the time in an invisible way without many knowing about them. The damage caused is diffused to the society and the soceity does not ordinarily treat them as crimes.
4. Memory, expansion, comprehension, critical analysis and intuitiveness are needed to commit the crime successfully.
5. Crimes are committed by people who matter in society. They are not committed by the ordinary **"Mortals"**.
6. They are not defined as crimes or offences in any Penal Codes and it is not possible to do so as the people who commit the crimes are able to manage and manipulate everything intelligently to their favour.
7. For many, instinctual crimes are ***"crimes proper"*** and crimes of intelligence are ***"virtues"*** for the people and society at large.

Owing to many reasons stated above and many other reasons, people do not or are not inclined to treat them as crimes. As such, those who commit such crimes do not have any guilt feelings or remorse for the criminal acts/omissions they do.

FORMATION OF EGO FACTOR *VIA* INTELLIGENCE

ANIMALITY (instincts) is the foundation over which the **Intelligence, Morality/Ethics and Spirituality** are constructed. With the foundation, the human mind is a single structure-forming an **ego factor.** How? It may be clearly understood that the evolution from animals to man is a frog jump with morality/ ethics, spirituality and intelligence. Animals are free to commit anything according to their instincts whereas the man cannot. His instincts are controlled by morality/ethics, spirituality and intelligence. Yet, man behaves from his instincts and any behaviour beyond a certain level (limit) is considered to be a crime and it is made so by morality/ethics, spirituality or intelligence and in many cases by two or more or by all. The **Ego Factor** is the mixture of all in one and it is this **Ego Factor** which behaves in a particular situation. Every human behaviour has its roots in **Instincts.**

Illustrations

Let us see how theft becomes a purely traditional crime and then an intellectual crime. Theft by definition is: Sec. 378 I.P.C.-1860 "Whoever intending to take dishonestly any movable property out of the possession of any person without that person's consent, moves that property in order to such taking, is said to commit theft.

Explanation 1—A thing so long as it is attached to the earth, not being moveable property, is not the subject of theft, but it becomes capable of being the subject of theft as soon as it is severed from the earth.

Explanation 2—A moving effected by the same act which effects the severance may be a theft.

Explanation 3—A person is said to cause a thing to move by removing an obstacle which prevented it from moving or by separating it from any other thing, as well as by actually moving it.

Explanation 4—A person, who by any means causes an animal to move, is said to move that animal, and to move everything which, in consequence of the motion so caused, is moved by that animal.

Explanation 5—The consent mentioned in the definition may be express or implied, and may be given either by the person in possession, or by any person having for that purpose authority either express or implied."

Theft is a traditional crime seen from the birth of a man. Pickpocketing, burglary, cheating, criminal misappropriation of property, extortion, cheating etc. are related to theft in someway or other. They have instinctual aspects and the instinctual forces may be (i) acquisitiveness (emotion is a feeling of ownership), and (ii) self-assertion (emotion is a feeling of superiority). Now, this theft is converted to white collar crimes, nexus crimes, *Mafia* crimes, organized racketeering or syndicates etc. by the intelligence and it may be as follows:

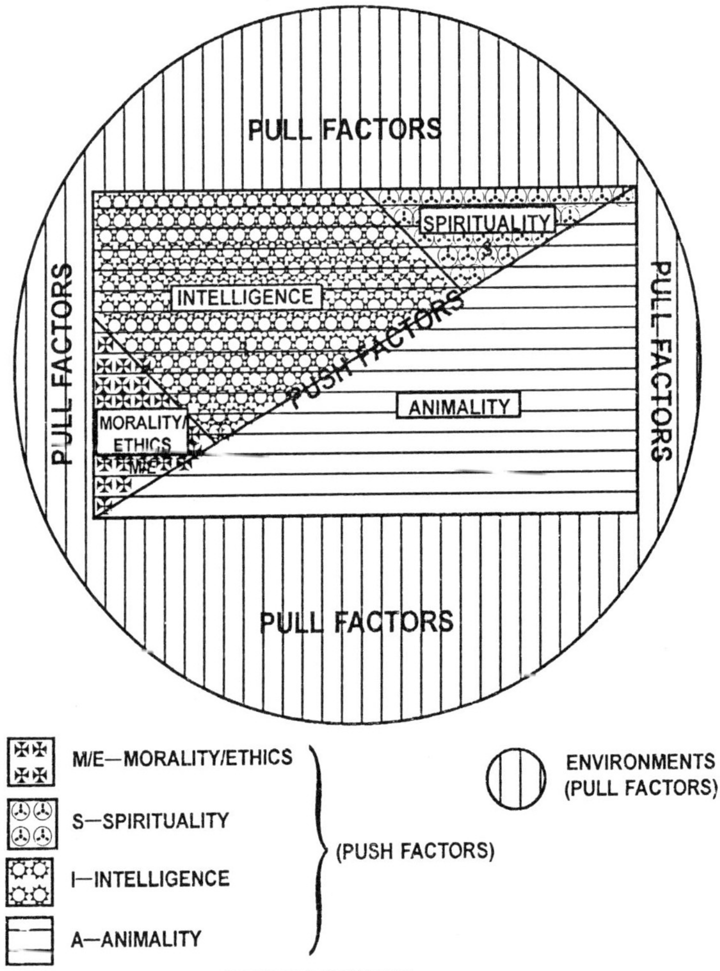

Fig. 4.1: Domination of INTELLIGENCE.

Here, in crimes where intelligence dominates, one may see that M/E (Morality/Ethics) and S (Spirituality) lie almost dormant there. In crimes like the white collar crimes, intelligence plays a major role in the planning and execution.

Why should the **intelligence** be developed in an upright way in the right direction? The reasons are many and different:

(i) Intelligence means the capacity for learning and understanding and similar forms of mental activities. The capacity for learning is developed on the basis of the opportunities provided (Pull Factors) and the intelligence of a Maoist is developed by providing situations for developing Maoist philosophy. Hence, to develop the intelligence uprightly in the right direction, one should provide such right thinking situations (Pull Factors).

(ii) Intelligence is related to brain. Brain washing means (a) a method for systematically changing attitudes or altering beliefs, originated in totalitarian countries especially through the use of torture, drugs, or psychological stress techniques; and (b) any method of controlled systematic indoctrination especially one based on repeatation or confusion. Terrorists, insurgents, fundamentalists, fanatics, and extrimists may be the products of brainwashing.

(iii) Intelligence may be developed in the right direction/ wrong direction. How to decide the right and wrong? The M/E (Morality/Ethics Ego) and the S (Spirituality Ego) may be of great use here. It is here we insist on the importance of good parents, good family, good neighbourhood, good schools, good value-oriented institutions, good religious teachings, good value promoting agencies, good media exposure, good information sources etc. Intelligence is to be developed in morality as well as in spirituality (Belief and Faith).

The question is: "Is the plundering of the property of the rich for distribution among the poor acceptable?" The intelligence will say "good or bad" depending upon its development uprightly in the right direction. A Naxalite may endorse the view that it is the right of the poor man to misbehave, plunder or extort the rich. According to him, the property belongs to the people and the rich have no justification to enjoy the wealth without giving it to the poor. According to him, the end justifies the means and his intelligence endorses the thinking fully. But a priest or a religious man will not accept

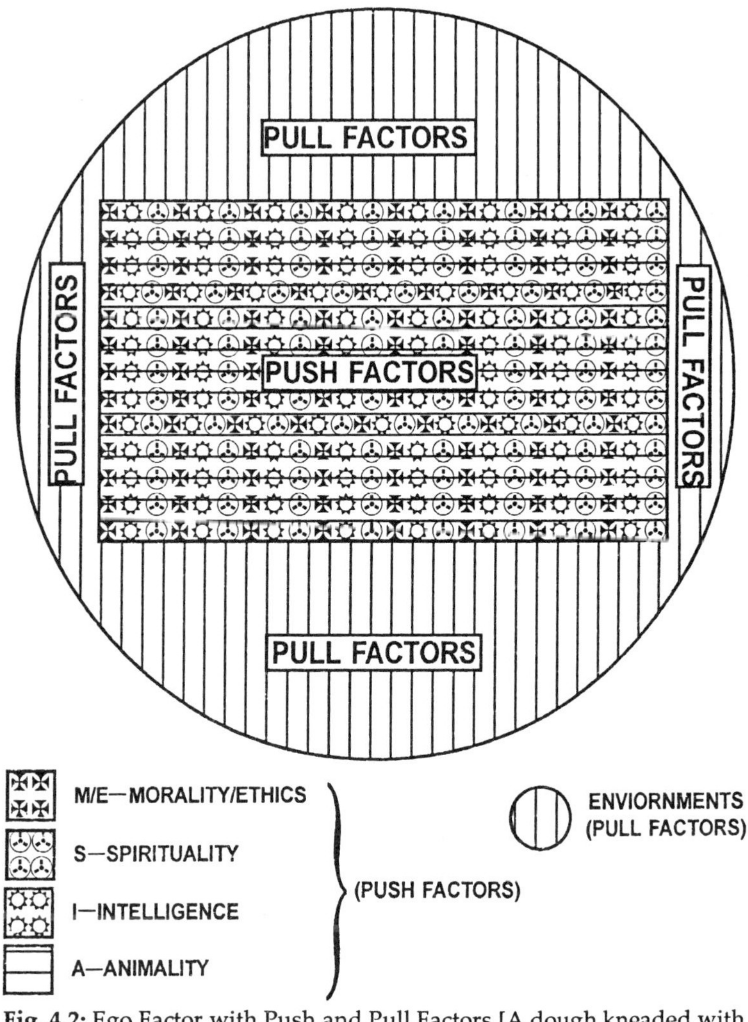

Fig. 4.2: Ego Factor with Push and Pull Factors [A dough kneaded with M/E, S, I & A].

such an intellectual interpretation. According to him both the end and the means must be justified. For him, it is better to starve and die rather than plundering the property of others.

The white collar criminals, nexus criminals, organized and ***Mafia*** criminals have their intellectual interpretations for everything they do. They may even say that the "morality is the lack of opportunity". According to them there is no means by which the human intelligence is uprightly developed in the right direction. Hence, they have an intellectual interpretation and explanation for every crime they commit. There is a justification for bribery, corruption, adulteration, illicit alcohol sale etc. and they provide intellectual explanations to support their views.

The intelligence (**Push Factor**) is developed on the basis of the **Pull Factors** (environments) given to each and every individual. Hence, the Ego Factor may be explained as shown in Fig. 4.2.

In the Fig. 4.2, the **Push Factors**-M/E, S and I with Animality interact with the **Pull Factors** (Environment) for the formation of an ego and an ego factor just like various powders are kneaded to make a dough. In other words, suppose that the—(i) Animality is the flower of rice; (ii) Intelligence is the flower of raggi; (iii) Morality/Ethics is the flower of wheat; and (iv) Spirituality is the flower of corn and they are kneaded in water to make special *chapati* (Indian Cookery, a flat pancake like bread, usually of whole wheat flour, baked on a griddle). The pure water is the pull factor (Environment) here and the result will be a dough of all flours. Depending upon the quantity of the flour put, the taste will be different. For example—

> 60 per cent wheat with 10 per cent corn, 10 per cent raggi and 20 per cent rice, then the taste of wheat will be projected in such a special *chapati*. Instead, if the 60 per cent is corn flour, its taste will be different.

Hence, depending upon the dominance of A, M/E, S or I, the behaviour will be different. An overdominance of A will result in a crime. Again, an overdominance of M/E will result in a highly moral/ethical act for the one who behaves and the overdominance of S will result in a highly spiritual act. In any case, any dominance beyond a limit will become abnormal, but need not necessarily be criminal violating the criminal laws. *Sati* (a Hindu practice whereby a widow immolates herself on the funeral pyre of her husband—now abolished by law), Harakiri, also called **Seppuku,** ceremonial suicide by ripping open the abdomen with a dagger or knife, formerly practiced in Japan by members of the warrior class when disgraced or sentenced to death—were not considered as criminal once upon a time. Why? The **Ego Factor** formed as a result of the interaction between the **Push** and **Pull Factors** was such that no one thought it to be a crime. Nevertheless, the intelligence (I) explained the foolishness of such acts so much so that *Sati* and Harakiri are treated as unacceptable and abnormal now.

Hence, for man it is necessary to have an intellectual conviction of what he does and thus, it is the reason why the scientists say that the **intelligence** is a **factor** which distinguishes human behaviour from animal behaviour. Next chapter is about **Morality/Ethics** as a factor controlling human behaviour.

Notes

1. Rational means "agreeable to reason, endowed with the faculty of reason, pertaining to or constituting reasoning powers" (Webster's).
2. Comprehend means "to understand the nature or meaning of ; grasp with the mind; perceive" (Webster's).
3. Expansion means increasing in extent, size, volume, scope etc., to spread or, expand or stretch out (Webster's).
4. Intuitiveness means direct perception of truth, fact etc., independent of any reasoning process; a keen and quick insight (Webster's).

5
Morality: A Factor Controlling Human Behaviour

Man is moral/ethical and this morality/ethics is seen in all people everywhere. People speak about (1) Absolute morality, (2) Relative morality. They also speak about (1) Subjective morality, and (2) Objective morality. No one speaks about a concept known as "No morality" for human beings. Animals, birds, reptiles, fishes and insects have no morality. I wrote a book titled POLICE MORALITY and I wrote the book as I found that some police officials were immoral in their attitude and approach. They had a subjective morality as they had the mindset as "I am O.K. and you are not O.K. morally." In police sub-culture I saw that the police officials were very much concerned only with **'Legal Sanity'** and not all with **'Moral Sanity'** when they talked about their interaction with the public. According to many, police officials ought not worry about the **'Moral Insanity'** whereas they should be well extra-ordinarily aware of the **'Legal Insanity'**.

It may be reiterated that the animals, birds, insects, reptiles and fishes are activated to bahave the way they do because of the instincts in them. These instincts are expressed in a naked way by them. Owing to their survival instincts, one animal pounces upon another and some times kills the victim. Might is the right in the animal kingdom whereas in the human kingdom, the might cannot and will not be always the acceptable mode of behaviour. There is morality and moral principles are there to guide or they must guide human behaviour.

Small fishes are eaten by the big ones and the same behavioural patterns are shown by birds. Vultures eat chicken and chickens eat worms. Man cannot and do not do so with people because he is guided by moral principles or morality. Sex is an instinct and animals express it basing on the odour. The dogs have the sexual odour-I have noticed their copulation in the months of September-October during which period they have the mating season. Likewise, I have taken note of snakes having their copulation/matings during the months of October-November. Cocks mate with any hens and they do several times during a day with all hens whenever or wherever possible. Man cannot do so as he is guided by morality or moral principles. There is marriage for him and thus one notices polygamy or monogamy, polyaundry etc. He cannot have sex with anyone and if he does so he will be punished or he will have guilt feelings or will be looked down upon.

Escape is an instinct and animals escape when they see any dangerous situations. Man cannot and does not do so. He may face any dangerous situation on moral grounds. I have any number of examples to show human beings suffering death or prefer to undergo any dangers on moral basis. Man has specific roles to perform in life and the role is given, some times, on moral grounds. Euthanasia is not favoured by many on moral grounds just to escape from the hardships connected with old age or ailments and sufferings. Abortions are disfavoured by many on the basis of morality. Moral laws are honoured as the laws written on human conscience and whenever one does it he may suffer from guilt conscience or will have unsettling of human mind.

People speak about subjective morality and objective morality. Accordingly, they use the words **"Ethics"**[1] and **"Morality"**. "Ethics", according to me, is the moral principle a person subjectively has whereas "Morality" contains the principles which a society keeps up. As such we speak about "Personal Ethics" and "Social Morality". Professional ethics is the moral principle to be followed by people following a particular profession and in all such situations, it is or must be congruent with the social morality-principles followed by the people in a society. At the ultimate level, in my view, the Ethics and Morality are or ought to be one and the same. Animals, birds, fish, reptiles and insects do not have ethics and morality. They have instincts and instincts are expressed without respecting any ethical and moral principles. For example, pugnacity (combat) is an instinct having anger as the accompanying emotion. Dogs fight on a bone and they do not show any concern when they fight each other. Man too has pugnacity, but he does not express it whenever or wherever he wants it to be expressed. Even in war, there are moral principles and the International Conventions are there to control the pugnacity of man during the war. Why? In morality and ethics, we have ***Norma Normans*** and ***Norma Normata.***

Norma Normans and Norma Normata

Every moral or ethical principle is a norm of behaviour. In that way the moral/ethical principles should be absolute, universal and eternal. For example: "You shall respect your parents." This is a principle law[2] from the time of Hammurabi (18th century B.C. or earlier, king of Babylonia) and the same is seen in the **Ten Commandments** given by God to **Moses** (The Hebrew prophet who led the Israelites out of Egypt and delivered the Law during their years of wandering in the wilderness.). It is a moral principle and is seen from time immemorial. It is believed to be universal and absolute as no one can change it. It is written in the human conscience of every man. Penal laws enacted by man may change; social laws may change; cultural laws may change, but moral laws cannot be changed as they are eternal and everlasting. The **Norma Normata** speaks about the principle behind the **Norma Normans** or the norming norm—i.e., the moral law. Why should the morality insist that "You shall respect your parents?" The law is in the human conscience and the foundation is very strong. The reasons or the arguments for such a moral law remain to be the same from the birth of man or humanity. It is a law of obligation of children to their parents. People who speak of subjective morality fail or refuse to accept this eternal truth.

I said earlier that the personal ethics might be different from the social morality. I insist to say that the ethics and morality must be one and the same. Some people may justify their actions on the basis of an ethical law which is purely subjective for them. *"It is the right of the poor man to misbehave, success through the barrel of the gun, the end justifies the means etc."* may be ethical principles for them. Nevertheless, they cannot be the moral principles. Ethical principle may make a man not to feel guilty even when he commits a morally wrong act. For example, abortion may be ethically justified by some whereas it is morally unjustified by others. Why? People who follow subjective morality may have their arguments to justify their otherwise objectively immoral acts.

Some moralists speak of relative morality. According to them, the morality is purely subjective and no one has any authority to question the right of a man when he makes an ethical/moral decision. If one's acts/omissions give him mental satisfaction/no guilt feelings, then the act/omission is morally justified for him. Suicide may be a morally/ethically justifiable act for such people. Use of third degree methods (i.e., intensive questioning or rough treatment, especially by police in order to get information or a confession) on suspects in a crime may be justifiable act for them. Some people push their old and infirm parents to old age homes and they do not have any guilt feelings.

There are people who subscribe to the view that morality and ethics may be nothing but lack of opportunity. What do they mean by such a statement? It means that one can afford to be an opportunist. This is otherwise called an "opportunist's ethics or personal morality." This is also known as a sort of **convenient morality.** If the wind is to this side, take "this side morality/ethics and alternatively," if the wind is to the other side, then have an "other side morality/ethics." This is called **"opportunism"** and precisely, therefore, it is called **"selfish morality/ethics."**

In human life, the question arises: "Which is more important?—Existence? or Essence?[3]" If the answer is "Existence", then comes an 'Existentialist' morality/ethics[4]. People who accept "Existentialist morality/ethics" give weights only to the utilitatian existence and they may not have any guilt feelings when they murder all who have a vegetative existence or non-utilitarian existence. On the other hand, all those who value "essence" will desist from demolishing, destroying or annihilating anything/anybody having a non-utilitatarian/vegetative existence. They have high moral values and they feel guilty whenever they violate the laws relating to the essence of man.

MORALITY—ETHICS AND GUILT FEELINGS

A person who violates the moral/ethical laws will have guilt feelings—a feeling that "something wrong" has been done and thus his/her mind is disturbed. I had practised some time in a psychotherapy clinic where people suffering from psychic disorders were treated. I could see a number of people who suffered from guilt feelings—to the extent of neurotic guilt feelings or delusional guilt feelings. The psychotherapist there was not a psychiatrist and therefore, he had recourse only to hypnotic therapy or psychoanalytic treatment. After a few years' service in that psychotherapy clinic, I came to a conclusion that many a psychoneurotic disorder had the base on guilt feelings. Once the guilt feeling is washed off by the psychotherapist, the patients got relief or cure as the case might be. I learnt from my therapeutic experience that human mind has **Morality/Ethics** as a strong part of their **Mind.**

MAN AND HIS MORAL/ETHICAL MIND

Any man has both a moral mind and an ethical mind. He accepts an absolute morality which is eternal, universal and everlasting. He also accepts personal ethics which is purely individualistic in nature, but linked to universal, absolute and eternal morality.

Illustration

1. A accepts that theft is a moral wrong, but he commits theft because he has no other option, but to commit theft and he claims that he is ethically right.
2. B admits that murder is a moral wrong, but he commits murder for self-defence and hence, he argues that he is ethically right.

No one desists from committing a crime for want of reasons and justifications. He may convince everyone that he did a right thing. The question is: "Can he convince his own conscience that he did the right thing ethically and morally"? "A psychopath" is a person who does not have any guilt feelings, i.e., lacking an ethical/moral mind—even when he commits a sin, a wrong, a vice, an offence, an antisocial act, a crime etc. 'People violate norms'. For, no norm except the moral norms is universal and unchanging. Studies conducted by me show that many of the offenders handled by the police, prosecutors and courts are not psychopaths or moral morons. They do suffer from guilt consciousness.

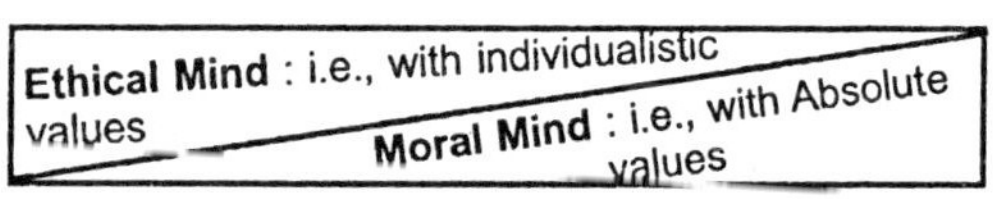

Fig. 5.1: Human Mind with Ethical and Moral Values (Man has an ethical) (individualistic) part and a moral part (universal) part in his mind).

I conducted a study on 306 murderers convicted for life imprisionment in Kerala State. I found out that majority of the life convicts in the prisons had guilt feelings and in some, the feelings were severe or profound. I got my research findings published and I strongly recommended that all who showed such a symptom ought to be released prematurely as they needed no more incarceration in a Centre for Personality Development (Prison).

FUNCTIONS OF THE ETHICAL AND MORAL MIND IN CRIMINALITY OR IN CRIMINAL BEHAVIOUR

In psychoanalytic school founded by Sigmund Freud (1856-1939, Austrian neurologist and the founder of psychoanalysis), he spoke about **ego, super ego and ID**. Ego means, as pointed out in the preface of this book, (i) the "I" or self of any person; a person as thinking, feeling, and willing, and distinguishing itself from the selves of others and from objects of its thought (Webster's). In Psychoanalysis, Ego means the part of the psychic apparatus that experiences and reacts to the outside world and thus mediates between the primitive drives of the 'id' and the demands of the social and physical environment. *Superego* in Psychoanalysis means, according to Webster's, the part of the personality representing the conscience, formed in early life by internalization of the standards of parents and other models of behaviour. 'id' in psychoanalysis means the part of the psyche, residing in the unconscious, that is the source of instinctive impulses that seek satisfaction in accordance with this pleasure principle and are modified by the ego and the *super ego* before they are given overt expression (Webster's).

Super ego, according to Freud, was the Do's and Don't, in the mind. In other words, it consisted of the laws, rules, regulations, customs and traditions, culture etc. which controlled the ID impluses? In **Push-pull-ego factor** theory the **moral part** of the mind is what is said to be the **super ego** in Freudian psychology. Eric Bearn spoke about **parent ego, adult ego** and **child ego.** The **parent ego** consisted of the laws, rules, regulations etc. which are otherwise seen in Freudian **super ego.** It may be noted that the **parent ego** had a controlling effect on the **child ego** which consisted of everything seen in Freudian **ID**. In **Push-pull-ego factor** approach, the **morality/ethics** part contains or consists of everything seen in the **parent ego** of Eric Bearn's Transactional Analysis (T.A.). The demonological theory in criminology (Pre-scientific theory of crime causation) brought the concept of an invisible **demon-satan-devil** as the cause of crime. In other words, the **demon** (Devil or Satan) was the **ID** of Freud, **child** of Eric Bearn and **animality** of **push-pull-ego factor theory.**

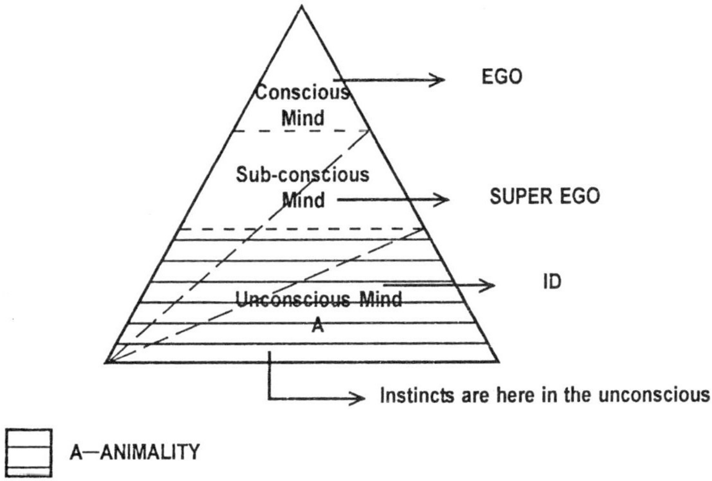

Fig. 5.2: Sigmund Freud's Mind Containing Ego, Super Ego and ID.

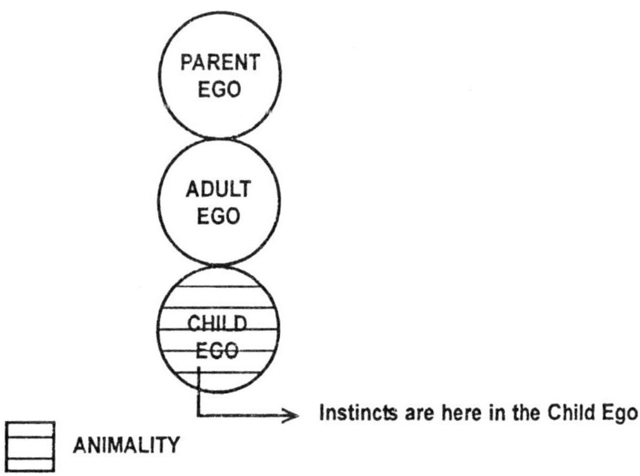

Fig. 5.3: Eric Bearn's Mind Containing Parent Ego, Adult Ego and Child Ego

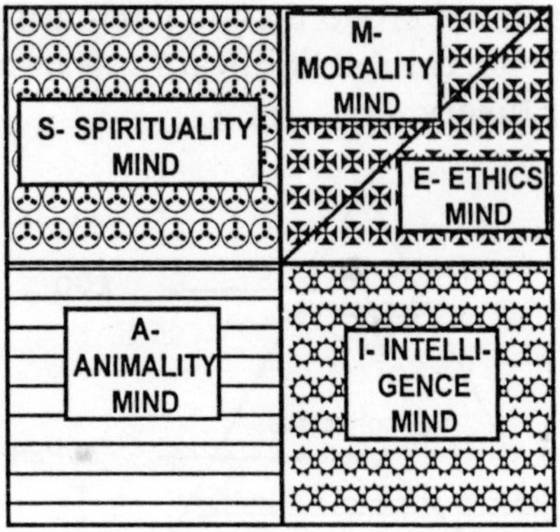

Fig. 5.4: Vadackumchery's **Push-pull-ego factor** theory of crime causation containing **ethical** and **moral** parts along with **animality, intelligence and spirituality.**

According to Sigmund Freud, the **super ego** controls the **ego** and thus the **ID** impulses are kept under control. He says further that an inadequate formation of super ego would make a person to commit crimes. According to Eric Bearn, a transaction could be transferred from Child Ego to Parent Ego and thus a complimentary transaction could be ensured. If it is not done, then a conflicting transaction would be resulted which could be a criminal act. In demonology, the Demon causes crime and God alone will be able to control the Demon and the man can get God's blessings, favour and graces *via* prayers and adoration to get out of the demonological instigation or influence. The **Push-pull-ego factor** theory too speak about the controlling power of the **ethical and moral part.** The theory says that Animality + Spirituality + Ethics/ Morality + Intelligence together form the **push factors** for the **ego** to behave. How do they do and how does it cause crime is a topic of discussion in the chapters that follow.

Ego formation is as under. Take water in a bottle. This is pure water and I may call it **animality** in man, i.e., the instincts.

Add to it some water which is coloured (say, green) and shake it. I may call it **spirituality,** i.e., the Beliefs and Faith.

Add to it some water which is coloured (say, red) and shake it. I may call it **intelligence,** i.e., the mental capacities/functions such as Memory, Comprehension, Expansion, Critical Analysis and Intuitiveness/Inventiveness.

Add to it some water which is coloured (say, blue) and shake it. I may call it **morality/ethics**, i.e., the Guilt or No Guilt feelings when an act is done or omitted.

Now, we may get coloured water which is not pure—not green—not red—not blue. The colour will be a new colour and it becomes the **push factors** in man. These **push factors** come into being after an interaction with the **pull factors** which are many in number. In fact, the **ego factor** is formed as a result of the interaction between the **push factors** and the **pull factors.** How? At a given time, a particular mind (ego) will dominate. If the dominating ego is **animality**, then a crime is likely to be committed. If the dominating ego is **spirituality**, then no crime is committed/or an abnormal behaviour which is treated as a crime is committed as one sees in human sacrifice to please God. If the dominating ego is **intelligence**, then no crime is committed. If the dominating Ego is **morality/ethics** then a crime may be committed—depending upon the moral/ethical principle one has.

When I teach **Push-pull-ego factor** theory, my students invariably ask me to make a distinction between **ethics and morality.** As stated earlier, **ethics** is individualistic whereas **morality** is universal. Ethics is relative, morality is absolute. Ethics may change while morality cannot. Ethics is time specific whereas morality is eternal. Today's ethics may not be there tomorrow while morality is everlasting from the birth of humanity to the consummation of the world. If one violates **ethics or morality** he will invariably suffer from guilt conscience. If one does not have such a guilt conscience, then he is rightly called a psychopath.

I have visited prisons several times and interviewed the prisoners. A book in Malayalam titled ***Kolapathakikalude Pinnamburam***, i.e. **Behind the Murderers** was published. During the course of my research to study the prisioners, I could learn that most of the murderers convicted for life sentence had **guilt conscience** and they expressed their guilt feelings both in the ethical way and in the moral way. They said:

1. *"I have no guilt feeling for killing my unfaithful and treacherous wife* **(Ethical Expression),** *but I have strong guilt feeling for becoming a murderer in life. Murder is a sin and an unforgivable act* **(Moral Expression)."**
2. A pick-pocket was interviewed and he told me that he had no regrets and did not feel guilty **(Ethical Expression)** and said that he picked the pockets of only the rich and the affluent. Precisely therefore, he did not have any guilt conscience **(Moral Expression).** I think that he was a psychopath.

I have seen rapists who felt acute guilt conscience for destroying the life of a girl. I have seen convicts who knew well that they have done a wrong, but never had any guilt feelings although they admitted the ethical and moral aspects of the wrongs they have done. No doubt, they had psychic problems and personality disorders. People who are theists or agnostics may be good moralists. There was a time during the development of criminological thoughts that many moralists came forward to explain the causes of crime and they argued that people committed crimes owing to moral deterioration. Even today, such moralists come forward with their favourite theories. During the pre-scientific period and the period between the classical and positive schools, some spiritual men and theologians came forward with their crackpot theories to explain the etiology of crime. All of them emphatically spoke about a **Moral Mind** and the educational system in many countries inculcate moral values during their education. They put **"Values and Moral Values"** in the syllabi of young children and moral value oriented education is given a lot of importance in schools and academic institutions of learning.

Here are some of the ethical and moral values and Table 5.1 gives a few of them. One may add more to the existing list.

Table 5.1: Ethical and Moral Values.

	Ethics[5] (Individual)		Morality[6] (Society)
1.	Professional ethics	1.	Absolute morality
2.	Lawyer's ethics	2.	Relative morality
3.	Policeman's ethics	3.	Excusable morality
4.	Ethics of war	4.	Opportunist's morality
5.	Judge's ethics	5.	Justifiable morality
6.	Media ethics	6.	Eternal morality
7.	Crime doer's ethics	7.	International morality
8.	Business ethics	8.	Time-being morality
9.	Trade ethics	9.	Gender morality
10.	Bureaucratic ethics	10.	Victim morality
11.	Domestic ethics	11.	Administrative morality
12.	Priestly ethics	12.	Judicial morality
13.	Correctional ethics	13.	Regional morality
14.	Criminal's ethics	14.	Linguistic morality
15.	Politician's ethics	15.	Political morality
16.	Gynec ethics	16.	Religious morality
17.	Child ethics	17.	Group morality
18.	Suspect's ethics	18.	Police morality
19.	Arrestee's ethics	19.	Racial morality
20.	Prisoner's ethics	20.	Sex morality
21.	Consumer ethics	21.	Old age morality

ETHICS AND MORALITY IN INDIVIDUALS, GROUPS AND SOCIETY

Morality and moral principles do not come into existence one day, too soon. Every morality/moral principle is centuries old—millenium old—seen from the birth of humanity. Hence, the morality/moral principles are transmitted from generations to generations—and it means that they are time immemorial. Social laws are laws made and enforced for the smooth running of the society and are the laws applicable *hic et nunc*. Cultural laws are the laws transmitted from generations to generations. No one knows when or where such cultural laws originated, but are seen powerfully operating even now. State-made laws are the laws which the Government in power has enacted to control the people. Religious laws are laws made and enforced after a particular religion had come into being. Divine or man-made, the religious laws are in force in society and people meticulously follow them. Institutional laws are the laws which human institutions have enacted for the smooth functioning of the institutions. Personal laws are there for each and every individual and they are needed for the harmonions living together in a society. Traditional laws are there to maintain the traditions of each society. Customary laws are there to keep up the customs of a society. And the **moral laws** are there to judge the **"Right** and **Wrong"** of every human act. Precisely, therefore, every law enumerated has or should have **moral foundation.** If the moral base is lost, the laws get themselves changed to establish the morality in society. Human mind has a **moral sphere** just like it has an **intellectual sphere, spiritual sphere** and **instinctual sphere.** All laws, rules, regulations, customs and traditions lie in the **moral sphere** of the human mind. Even spiritual laws should have a moral base.

MORAL MIND AND ANIMAL INSTINCTS

It may be repeated that man cannot act without instincts and he cannot act just like the fish, insects, birds, reptiles and animals behave instinctively. Human behaviour is controlled by his **Intelligence, Morality, Ethics and Spirituality.** Morality speaks about the "Right and Wrong" of human act.[7] All instinctual acts/omissions cannot be treated or considered as **"Right"** in human kingdom. Individuals, groups and society should exist, live and survive only on moral principles, i.e., **right** or **wrong** and it is decided on the laws operating in the human kingdom. An animal can kill a man and it did so instinctively whereas a man cannot. An animal may eat as much as it wants without showing any consideration to other animals. Man has control over all animals, birds, reptiles and fish etc. on earth—thus, is seen in Scriptures, but he cannot exert such controls on human beings as he is controlled by Moral Laws. Today we see Human Rights Justice, Victim Justice, Social Justice, Gender Justice, Equal Justice, Caste Justice, Race Justice, Linguistic Justice, Regional Justice, Criminal Justice, International Justice etc. and they have their roots on **Morality and Moral Justice**. I have enumerated more than 48 types of justice and all of them have their base on **Morality and Moral Justice**. Any law without a moral basis will never be a law. Hence, human mind has a **Moral Sphere.**

MORAL MIND DEVELOPMENT

How does the **Moral Mind** develop in the neonate? I have observed the development of the **Moral Mind** *via* a number of stages during its **Ego** (Personality) development. The six stages may be:

1. First Stage

Up to 6-7 months. The child needs its physiological needs satisfied. Whenever it feels hungry, it cries immediately. The child is fed by its loving and caring mother. Whenever the child has any physiological discomforts like the feeling of too much coldness/heat etc., the child cries and the mother comforts the child by appropriate methods (like, putting a blanket on its body, switching on the electric fans/air-conditioner etc.) and thus the infant realizes or internalizes the moral truth that caring, looking after, having concern to others etc., are necessary for human beings for their proper development. The infant needs the care and concern of the mother (parents) for fulfilling its physiological and psychological needs. If not, the development of the Moral Mind will be defective to that extent.

2. Second Stage

Up to 18-20 months. During this stage, the child looks around and realizes that there are many more people around it. The infant is fed primarily with mother's milk and the bodily touch of the mother with the infant makes it to have the feeling that it is cared and looked after well. However, the child starts reacting to the mother by biting the nipple when it feels difficulties to get the breast-milk. If the breast-feed is not enough, the child is given extra food. The infant develops the sense of caring and concern more. The child is bathed and the child internalizes the moral and social needs to have cleanness in life. Concurrently, the **spiritual** as well as the **intellectual minds** too get developed. The interactions between the infant and the mother, parents, family members decide how good or bad the sense of morality and spirituality develops in the developing child. During this period, a give and take sense too is developed and it is found to be very essential to have such a moral sense developed in the growing children.

3. Third Stage

18-20 months to 40-42 months (up to 3½ years). This is the period the child spends time with siblings, if any, parents and others. The child goes to the nursery classes afterwards. Hence, for interpersonnel (personal) relationship and moral/social norms to be kept, adjustment with others at home, cooperating, assisting and co-existing with all at home etc. are internalized. The child develops a sense of initiative. Concurrently, the spiritual and intellectual minds too are developed. Language is learnt and starts talking fluently with words. What are morally and socially acceptable to the family members?—they learn them now. This is a period of developing non-verbal signals to communicate with others. Lack of encouragement or support from parents/family members may have bad or undesirable effect/impact on the development of the **Moral, Social, Interpersonnel** (Personal) **and Spiritual** spheres of the developing child.

4. Fourth Stage

Up to 40-42 months to 14 years. The child goes to school and its interpersonnel (personal) relations and social contacts are extended. More and more moral, social, cultural and interpersonnel (personal) values are internalized, the child develops a sense of accomplishments. The child acquires knowledge and skills and further learns to co-operate, assist and develop harmonious co-existence with a world of friends, elders and juniors, teachers and others around the neighbourhood, community, social and religious organizations etc. The child develops further a sense of accomplishment. The moral sense is further widened. The child gets opportunites to have access to publications, media and learning materials both at schools and outside. Morality and moral sense may be strengthened. The family, especially the parents, schools, neighbourhood community, social and religious organizations have to play positively for the development of moral values in an upright way in the right direction and thereby to develop the personality and the **Ego Factor** in the growing child. By this time, the child, as a rule, crosses puberty and it is seen that the ground work or the foundation is well laid down for proper and further development of **Ego** and **Ego Factor.**

From the birth of a child, one sees the instincts playing their role in many ways. While the instincts are needed for activation, the excessiveness or the overactivation is not warranted for the proper development of the personality of the child. The success in moral development is seen in the inculcation of the right moral values in an upright way in the right direction. Sigmund Frued spoke about the development of the sex instincts up to puberty. In my studies, I have observed the development of all animal instincts and the attempt is to make or convert the animal instincts to **human drives**—morally/ethically, spiritually and intellectually.

5. Fifth Stage

Up to 14 years to 35 years, i.e., from puberty to adulthood. Of course, there is a period of adolescence, i.e., 17 to 19 years—and during the fifth stage, an individual constructs the superstructure over the **foundation** already built up. He has education, exposure, entertainment, contacts and thoughts about his future, plans and thus he/she becomes more and more matured in the personality, attitudes, approaches *'....osophies'*, *'......isms'* and *'....ologies'*. His moral sense is developed and his instincts come under control. As a result, maturity in emotions is seen. Hence, in Malayalam, there is a saying. "At the age of 20, **WHAT.....?**" "...and at the age of 40, full maturity" which means that the emotions get fully matured by the time a person becomes 40 years of age.

6. Sixth Stage

Up to 35 years and upwards. Maturity in morality and moral sense is seen in all activities. Give and take attitude may be shown. People who had inadequate instinctual development or emotional control during the previous stages are likely to show such immature behaviour even at this stage. Such people tend to commit crimes even at this stage. My conclusion is that a positive movement through all stages is the basis for normal **Ego Factor** development. In other words, the Morality/Ethics Potencies, Spirituality Potencies, Intellectual Potencies and Animality (Instincts) Potencies will develop (i.e., the **Push Factors**) in an upright way in the right direction if and only if the **Push Factors** are really very positive and proper. This is shown in Fig. 5.5.

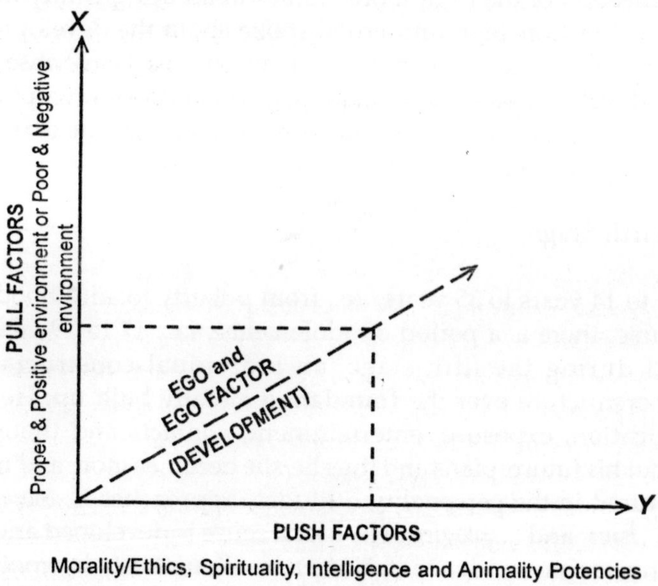

Fig. 5.5: Development of Ego and Ego Factor.

The more the proper and positive **Pull Factors,** the more will be their interaction with the **Push Factors** and the **Ego** and the **Ego Factor** will be then uprightly formed in the right direction. On the contrary, if the **Pull Factors** are poor and negative then the **Ego** and **Ego Factor** development will be defective to that extent and it may result in the commission of crimes.

MORALITY/ETHICS, INDIVIDUAL, GROUP AND SOCIETY

Elsewhere I said that the individual/subjective morality is called **ethics.**

Whenever a person commits a morally wrong act (omissions too), he becomes the best Counsel to argue his case to his favour. On the other hand, whenever another person commits a morally wrong act (omissions too), he becomes the best Judge to decide on the morality and/or immorality (Ethics too) of the act/omission—I used to say thus to my students at the Police Training College. I say so because I have seen the policemen employing third degree methods during interrogation. According to the Indian Penal Code, section 323 reads: *"Whoever, except in the case provided for by section 334, voluntarily causes hurt, shall be punished with imprisonment of either description for a term which may extend to one year or with fine which may extend to one thousand rupees, or with both".* This is applicable to any citizen on road. Now, read the section 330 I.P.C. which is applicable to the police officials, i.e., *"whoever voluntarily causes hurt for the purpose of extorting from the sufferer or from any other person interested in the sufferer, any confession or any information which may lead to the detection of an offence or misconduct, or for the purpose of constraining the sufferer or any person interested in the sufferer to restore or to cause the restoration of any property or valuable security or to satisfy any claim or demand or to give information which may lead to the restoration of any property or valuable security shall be punished with imprisonment of either description for a term which may extend to seven years, and shall also be liable to fine."* What do these two sections (S. 323

and S. 330 I.P.C.) speak about? One and the same act (Hurt here) is punished with one year's imprisonment and with seven years imprisonment depending upon who commits it. When the ordinary man on the street commits hurt, the policeman sees it as an offence—legally as well as morally. On the other hand, when the same act (Hurt) is committed by a policeman, the policeman does not or refuses to judge the act to be an offence (legally as well as morally). He is a good Advocate (Counsel) here on his act whereas he is the best Judge on the act of others.... Why? Here, one sees the difference between **Ethics** and **Morality**. Ethics which is subjective justifies the act, though it is criminal. Morality which is social, objective, absolute and eternal judges the same act to be criminal (moral wrong). Hence, one should accept the importance and significance of the **Ego Factor.** If the **Ego** is uprightly formed in the right direction, then it will judge the **hurts** in both cases to be criminal (morally wrong). In the development of the **Ego Factor** (personality), the **Pull Factors** are significantly important. If the **Ego Factor** is uprightly formed in the right direction, then one may not commit hurt in both situations and he will have guilt feelings if he violates the **Ego** norms. Hence, I may emphatically say: "If the personal ethics goes in conformity with the social morality when the **Ego** is formed and developed, it is the best way for an upright development of the **Ego Factor** in the right direction." Such a person will not commit immoral and/or illegal acts. An uprightly formed **Ego Factor** in the right direction is a **Buffer**, i.e., a device or mental apparatus used as a shield/bumper against commission of crimes.

Illustrations

1. A high caste Hindu may ethically justify untouchability although it is a moral wrong in a society. An **Ego** with one and the same ethical principle and moral principle will disapprove of untouchability as a desirable act. He will desist from committing untouchability. Untouchability in Hinduism means the quality or condition of being an untouchable in the Vedic

tradition to persons of low caste or to persons excluded from the caste system (Webster's).

2. *Racism (Racialism),* i.e., a belief or doctrine that inherent differences among the various human races determine cultural or individual achievement, usually involving the idea that one's own race is superior and has the right to rule others (Webster's). One sees in history the racial descrimination and apartheid in South Africa. Some people justified apartheid ethically while many objected to it morally. If the ethics and morality become one and the same, then that **Ego** Factor will control any criminal behaviour on the basis of racial discrimination.

What about the Group Ethics/Morality? Consider the groups like (1) *Fundamentalists,* i.e., those who have strict adherence to any set of basic ideas or principles, no matter they are ethical/unethical, moral/immoral etc. (2) *Extremists,* i.e., people with a tendency or disposition to go to extremes or an instance of going to extremes, especially in political matters. Examples may be leftist extrimism, the extrimism of the Naxalites, Maoists, Nazis etc. They have their own special or/ and specific ethics which may be different from the social morality. They may involve in the commission of a variety of crimes without any guilt feelings. (3) *Fanatics*—those with an extreme and an uncritical enthusiasm or zeal, as in religion or politics. They may say "No salvation beyond and besides..... religion" and they kill people professing other faiths or religious beliefs. They feel pleasant when they commit crimes to promote and propagate their religion/politics and their **Ego Factor** is thus formed, shaped or developed in a defective way. (4) *Terrorists,* i.e., persons who are generally members of a group who employ or advocate terrorism (Formerly, they were the members of a group in Russia aiming at the demoralization of the Government in power.) Terrorism means the use of violence and threats to intimidate or coerce especially for political purposes. The terrorists have an **Ego Factor** developed as a result of the interaction between the **Push** and **Pull Factors.** Therefore, they do not feel any guilt when they involve in terrorism. Their **Ethical Ego** justifies their acts fully as acceptable. The social **Morality** may be against their ethical conviction. (5) *Insurgents,* i.e., individuals who rise in forcible opposition to lawful authority, especially people who engage in armed resistance to Government or to the execution of its laws. The **Ego Factor** in such insurgents is the after effect of long interactions between the **Push** and **Pull Factors.** In Jammu & Kashmir, in Assam, in Jharkhand and other north Indian States in India, one sees a number of insurgent groups and they engage in armed combat with para-military forces. They take pride in their venture and have no guilt feelings as they have ethical justifications/rationalizations for what they do.

Coming to various groups engaged in many types of criminal activities, for example, the nexus criminals (those who have unholy linkage (nexus) with the bureaucrats, political leaders, businessmen and so on to commit crimes), the *Mafia,* i.e., hierarchically structured secret organization allegedly engaged in smuggling, racketeering, trafficking in narcotics and other criminal activities in U.S., Italy and elsewhere and in Kerala (India), one sees Local Level *Mafia,* Regional Level *Mafia,* State Level *Mafia* and in India, we may see Inter-State *Mafia* dealing with drugs, edibles, medicines, liquors and many such consumer items, one may take note of the fact that they have developed an **Ego Factor** without any guilt feelings and they have their ethical explanations. Investment *Mafia,* Visa *Mafia,* Employment *Mafia,* Money chain, Multi-marketing, Resorts *Mafia,* Flat *Mafia,* Cinema and T.V. Serial *Mafia,* Advertisement *Mafia,* Prayer *Mafia,* Healing *Mafia, Mantravada, Kudotram, Elas, Bhasma, Chatan Seva Mafias,* Pilgrim *Mafia,* Ayurveda Medicine *Mafia,* Massage *Mafia* and thus the list is very long. They have no guilt feelings as they have ethical consolation for what they do. Enforcement crimes, consensus crimes, corruption and bribery, sale of justice and services, white collar crimes, JEL crimes—all belong to this category.

Here, the Morality/Ethics dominates and between Morality and Ethics, the **Ethics** dominates. Precisely therefore, such groups involve in the commission of crimes without any guilt feelings. The members feel pride in committing crimes as the **Group Mind** and the **Group Ego Factor** accept the commission of crimes as desirable and acceptable.

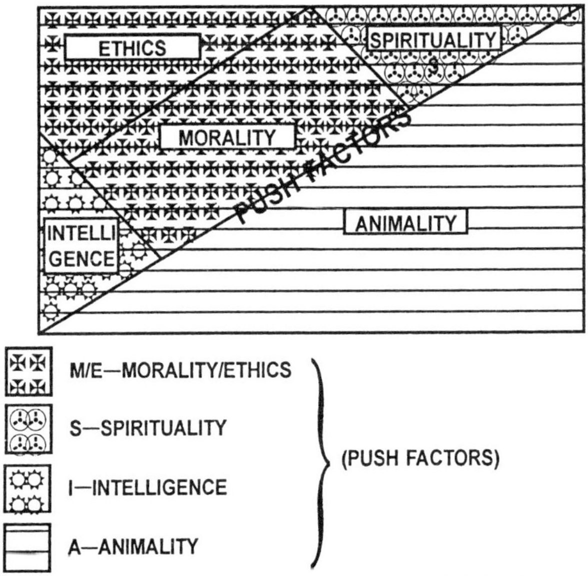

Fig. 5.6: Domination of Ethics of the human mind (M, I, S & A are relatively dominant).

What about the **Society Morality/Ethics?** Of course, there is an international community/society and the international society has a morality. International society accepts Murder, Rape, Theft, Robbery, Forgery, Extortion, Hurt etc. as morally wrong acts although some special and specific sub-society in the international society may ethically justify murder, plundering etc. Nevertheless, we may admit, as pointed out earlier, that there are internationally accepted moral principles and the violation of such principles will evoke international resistance to the violation of such principles. People evaluate every behaviour to be moral/ethical basing on international scales which are not usually changing. Hence, there is a school of thought which adheres to the view that morality is not relative. In other words, every act should be evaluated only in relation to international principles of morality and they are absolute and eternal. However, the criminal may have lot of ethical justifications for what he does. This is the reason why we see a lot of dimensions in justice administration beyond and besides the criminal justice. We have today, as indicated elsewhere victim justice, total justice, holistic justice, justice to the justice system, just justice and in one way or other all of them are related to moral/ethical principles which form the **Ego Factor** of a society as a whole.

Notes

1. Ethics in Webster's means "the rules of conduct recognized in respect to a particular class of human actions or a particular group, culture etc.: medical ethics, Christian ethics, moral principle as of an individual."
2. Code of Hammurabi, a Babylonian legal code instituted by Hammurabi and dealing with criminal and civil matters.
3. The basic real, and invariable natures of a thing or its significant individual feature or features.
4. Existentialism in philosophy is an attitude associated especially with Heidegger, Jaspers, Marcel and Sartre and opposed to rationalism and empiricism, that stresses the individual's unique position as a self-determining agent responsible for the authenticity of his or her choices.
5. Ethics may be personal.
6. Morality may be universal, absolute and eternal.
7. Morality means in Webster's "conformity to the rules of right conduct; moral and virtuous conduct. There is a branch called 'Moral Theology' dealing with the principles of moral conduct."

6
Spirituality: A Factor Propelling Human Behaviour Forward

Is man spiritual? The obvious answer to this question is *"yes, he is"*. Then how? Spiritual means incorporeal—super natural -ethereal—pertaining to the spirit as the seat of religious nature— something or sombody invisible to our naked eye. In the story of Adam and Eve, one sees the **satan** (devil or evil spirit) instigating Eve to eat the fruit of the **forbidden tree.** It is believed that there are legions of devils—very industrious spirits whose sole work is to instigate the weak to commit sins—i.e., transgression of divine law; violation of religious principles. No one knows why do they do so and make sinners to house in the hell where a devil called Lucifer[1] is the chief. True or false, millions of people down the millenia believed in the existence of evil spirits outside man living and prospering or successfully instigating the fragile mortal man to commit crimes/sins.

Again in the Holy Bible, one sees holy angels and guardian angels whose names are Raphael, Michael, Gabriel and so on. They are the archangels and in the New Testament, it is learnt that Angel Gabriel appeared to **MARY** to announce the birth of Jesus Christ. It is written in the Bible: "In the sixth month, the angel Gabriel was sent by God to a town in Galilea called Nazareth, to a virgin betrothed to a man named Jospeh, of the House of David; and the virgin's name was Mary. He went in and said to her: "Rejoice, so highly favoured! The Lord is with you". She was deeply distrubed by these words and asked herself what this greeting could mean, but the angel said to her, "Mary, do not be afraid; you have won God's favour. Listen! you are to conceive and bear a son, and you must name him Jesus. He will be great and will be called son of the Most High. The Lord God will give him the throne of his ancestor David, he will rule over the House of Jacob forever and his reign will have no end. Mary said to the angel. "But how can this come about since I am a virgin?" The Holy Spirit will come upon you, the angel answered "and the power of the Most High will cover you with its shadow. And so the child will be holy and will be called Son of God. Know this too: your kinswoman Elizabeth has, in her old age, herself conceived a son, and she whom people called barren is now in her sixth month, for *nothing is impossible to God.* I am the handmaid of the Lord, said Mary "Let what you have said be done to me and the angel left her" [St. Luke, 1:26-38, *Jerusalem Bible,* London] People down the centuries believed in the existence of Holy Spirits outside the man. Thus, one sees a spiritual world where holy and evil spirits live and survive. The belief in spirits among the people has been so intense that one cannot think of a world without spirits.

In people's talks, preacher's sermons, religious men's exhortations, cultural programmes (e.g., Shakespeare's dramas), black magics, occult practices, *mantravadas,* prayers to the Almighty, *Kudotram* etc., the belief in spirits and role of the spirits in controlling human behaviour may be observed.[2] By the advent of various religions around the world, belief in God, gods, in supernatural powers, evil spirits came into being. Man wanted a super natural Being for his existence and survival and he found or created such a super natural (spiritual) being outside him. There have been two schools of thought and they were:

(1) A school which argued that God created man in his own image.
(2) A school which argued that man created God in his own image.

The dispute is not settled even today as both schools have their own arguments and counter-arguments. In any case, it is accepted that God and men have the same **image.** Before established religions came into existence, people believed in the **power** of Nature and one sees gods like **fire** god, **water** god, **air** god and many such powers of nature. Those Natures' powers were given some shapes or other for the people to worship and adore them. Thus, one could see cruel animals' heads fitted with human bodies or fear causing birds with human body etc. all with a frightening look, teeth and eyes. People used to tremble before such gods of human imagination and in the Old Testament, Moses saw people adoring such man-created frightening gods when he was believed to have come down with **ten commandments** from the mount of **Senai.** In Hinduism, one could see gods seated on the back of cruel and wild carnivorous animals like lions, tigers etc. and some gods have fear causing faces. Among the tribal community, one sees no organized religions and religious gods. They have created their own gods for adoration and worship. Paganism, religion, theology, occult sciences, demonology, black magic, spiritualism etc. are topics of research and study in universities. Some people have belief even in human gods and there are living people who claim to be the incarnations of god on earth. Thus, the existence of a world of **spirits** and gods is seen outside the mortal man. There are theists, atheists, agnostics, humanists, rationalists, empiricists, existentialists, spiritualists and so on everywhere in the world. There exist prayers, adorations, occult practices, exorcism, sacrifice of people for divine pleasure, child sacrifice, penance taking, fasting to please gods, belief in life after death, belief in rebirth after death (*Punarjanma*), heaven, hell, purgatory, wandering souls after death, souls in bliss after death, declaration of saints in heaven, rituals and rubrics to please gods, visiting to pilgrim centres to get god's blessings, making offerings, worshipping snakes, Natures' powers etc., construction of temples, mosques, churches, gurudwaras, prayer centres, becoming priests, *pujaris*, prayermen, occult practitioners, reciting prayers, making spititual sermons and speeches, religious retreats, celebrating feasts and festivals, making offerings to gods and god men in various categories—with or without clothes, religious fundamentalism, religious fanaticism, communalism, religious terrorism, brutal murders in the name of gods etc., and to cut short it is often said that more murders in number have taken place in the name of gods and religions than in wars and such other things. Atrocities committed on man by man in the name of gods and religions are unimaginable and beyond human conception. All said and done, spirits, supernatural beings, gods and religions thrive and survive in some form or another and it is seen from the beginning of humanity and it will continue to be so till the death of humanity.

BELIEF AND FAITH IN SPIRITUALITY

Spiritual world is beyond human intelligence. Man's intelligence has nothing to do much with the spiritual power of man. Spirituality is beyond human intelligence as it is based on two concepts, namely **belief**[3] and/or **faith**[4]. What is **belief**? In my considered view, it is the invisible assurance which a man has when he wants to achieve a goal that he will achieve the goal. What is **faith**? This is the conviction which a man has in an invisible power which is supernatural. It can be the God, the gods, saints, angels and so on.

Both Belief and Faith are required for human beings to exist and survive. No man can live without them. Why? A person will have Belief as well as Faith in an invisible Being. Alternatively, a person can have Belief, but no Faith in a supernatural Being. A person who has Faith can have Belief as well. Hence, many a time people **mix faith** and **belief** and speak of them as one and the same. In many **creeds** of the religions, one sees **faith and belief** mixed together so much so that ordinarly a common man cannot isolate or distinguish **faith** from **belief** or **belief** from **faith.**

Illustrations

1. A humanist says **loving people** will bring prosperity

and happiness. He does as he believes. What is the assurance he has received to say so? Who has given him the assurance? No one has given him any assurance, yet he has the ardent **Belief** in what he says. At the same time, he does not have any **Faith** in a personal God/gods to say so.

2. A theist says **God will Reward** you for the love you give to the people. What is the assurance he has received to say so? Who has given him the assurance? No one has given any assurance, yet he has an ardent **Faith** in what he says.

In most of the cases, people have **Belief** and **Faith.** It may be noted that **Faith** is always with God or a supernatural Being or a Spiritual Entity in existence objectively for such people. On the other hand, **Belief** may be with a **Faith** in a personal God/gods/supernatural Beings/spiritual entity. Just like the **Moral and Ethical Mind** man has a **Spiritual Mind** and it may be drawn as a diagram as under. **Spiritual** here means **Invisible**—nothing more or nothing less.

BELIEF in an invisible assurance/assump- tions believed to be real	FAITH in a super natural power—a personal God/gods, spirit/s in objective existence

(Man has **Belief** and/or **Faith** as the spiritual parts in his mind)

Fig. 6.1: SPIRITUAL MIND with BELIEF and/or FAITH.

Since, **spiritual mind** is an integral part of the human mind just like Intelligence and Morality/Ethics, the **push factors** contain spiritual mind as well. In other words, **push factors** mean **Animality + Morality/Ethics + Spirituality + Intelligence** put together. For the development of **Intelligence,** we have educational institutions, universities, higher centres of research and development etc. For **Animality,** we have a number of establishments and institutions to satisfy the animal instincts like Hotels, Restuarants, Swimming pools, Maternity centres, Hospitals, Pleasure giving establishments like theatres, swimming pools, play grounds, stadia, indoor games etc. For **Morality/Ethics,** we have the control systems like the police, courts, prisons, punishments, home, media, charity institutions, moral value development centres, retreat centres, schools etc.

For **Spirituality,** we have churches, chapels, temples, mosques, synagogues, gurudwaras and some of such institutions and establishments are pilgrim centres—huge buildings of wonder in the world. If they are for **Faith,** then we have many organizations and institutions established for promoting and propagating **Belief.** Perhaps, the political parties in a democratic set-up, the non-governmental organizations (NGOs) with very noble ideas, charitable institutions like orphanages, homes for the aged and the infirm, mentally retarded and patients with psychic disorders, cancer patients, paliative care, houses for AIDs patients etc. work under *a belief that the Good Work Done* will be Rewarded. As said earlier, in many a case, the **Belief and Faith** go hand in hand together—in unison, so much so that many religions and religious workers, god-men, faithful do religious as well as charitable works. The number of men and women engaged in spiritual and charitable works run in millions and people get mental pleasures in being and becoming spiritual and charitable. A moral mind works behind such works.

MORALITY, ETHICS, SPIRITUALITY GIVE PLEASURE TO HUMAN MIND

Aesthetics[5] is a subject of study and we enjoy Beauty: Beauty gives pleasure to the human sense (Animality); to the **intelligence** if and only if it has meanings (memory), values (analysis), messages (intuitiveness) etc., to the **Morality/Ethical Mind** if and only if it has moral contents acceptable to the human intelligence; and to the **Spiritual Mind** if and only if it gives assurance to a better world order.

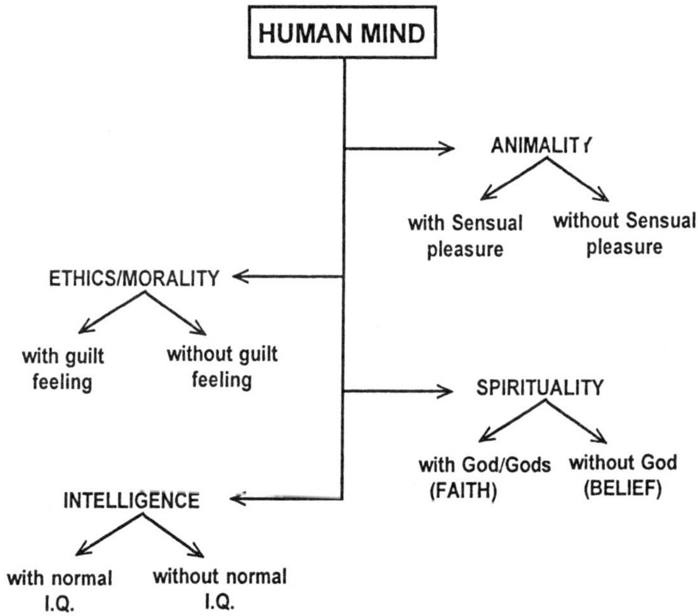

Fig. 6.2: Structure of the Human Mind.

HUMAN LAWS, MORAL LAWS AND DIVINE LAWS (RELIGIOUS LAWS)

While I was engaging a workshop at St. Thomas Apostolic Seminary, Kottayam, I raised a question to the seminarians there and it was: "what are the various categories of laws controlling a man"? I expected that they would answer the question saying—(i) social laws, (ii) cultural laws, (iii) ethical/moral laws, (iv) institutional laws, and (v) State made laws etc. But, to my surprise, they answered me telling (i) Human Laws, and (ii) Divine Laws. I asked them to tell me more about the Divine Laws which according to them were nothing, but God-made or

God given laws. They were candidates for priesthood in the Catholic church and therefore, I appreciated their views about God made/God given laws. They meant Religious Laws when they spoke about God made/God given laws. I asked them further to tell me: "Which are the God made/God given laws?" and they answered me saying about the Ten Commandments given to Moses by God at Mount Senai. I know that the Ten Commandments were the penal laws of Hammurabi (eighteenth Century B.C. or earlier king of Babylonia) who lived prior to Moses, the Hebrew prophet who led the Israelites out of Egypt and delivered the law during their years of wandering in the wilderness. As the people were not abiding by the then existed penal laws (as it is seen today too—that people violate the penal laws) the Biblical author gave a divine touch and authority for the people to accept and obey the then existed penal laws. Remember that the Ten Commandments were given by Moses to the people during the Exodus[6] and at a time he saw the people worshipping a man-made god. The first three commandments were, therefore, about God and worship and the rest seven were about controlling of crimes like murder, theft, giving false testimony, adultery and looking after parents etc. An invisible God (Yahweh, Elohim) at Mount Senai handed over to Moses the laws in two plates and they were called **Ten Commandments.** According to some Bible scholars, there were three sources from where the Biblical portion had come. They were Yahwistic source (the source named God as **Yahweh**), Elohistic source which called Him **Elohim** and Priestly source which addressed Him as God. No one except Moses saw God and Moses was an old man with a long beard and grey hairs exhibiting the maturity of age and authority. People trusted him and believed that the penal laws of Moses were the God made/ God given laws. When religions became organized, the religious authorities made many laws and they called them Divine laws, the violation of which was called **sin** and the punishment was given after the death of a man. The academicians and scholars started studying the etiological aspects of **sins** and thus one sees the demonological theories. Thomist approaches (1225?-'74), explanations given by *sadhus, sannyasis, pujaris,* priests, religious men, theologians, spiritual teachers and so on and thus a set of divine laws came into being. In the view of a criminologist, they are nothing, but 'man-made laws—religious laws'—for which the punishment is thought to be given by God after the death of a man in a spiritual world based on **Faith** or **Belief** or both as the case may be.

Those who did not have **Faith** in a God/gods' divinities, saints and so on had **Belief** in the moral laws/ethical laws. Moral laws are not divine laws, but are man-made laws to administer justice, equity and good conscience to people. As God is the punishment giver in divine laws, the **moral conscience** is the punishment giver when moral laws are violated. This is the reason why human intelligence says that the human conscience should be formed in an upright way in the right direction. There come justice, justness, equity and good conscience. Social laws are society made laws for the well-being and harmonious living together of the people living in the society. Cultural laws are culture-made and traditions and customs become important to maintain cultural pleasure and happiness. Institutional laws are made by institutions and personal laws are made by individuals. Thus, the moral/ethical mind of man is the reservior of all laws, no matter they are made by any agency—visible or invisible. This treasury of laws controls or should control the animality in man. Thus, one sees—

(1) Guiding and controlling of human behaviour done by the **Moral/Ethical Mind.**
(2) Progress to an end and hopefully proceeding to the goal are managed by the **Spiritual Mind.**
(3) The intelligent functions of human behaviour are controlled, guided and managed by the **Intellectual Mind.**

The foundation is always in the **Animal Mind** in which the instincts, i.e., the activating forces are seen. Thus, the **Push Factors** comprise of **Animality + Spirituality + Morality/Ethics + Intelligence.**

SPIRITUAL MIND, HOPE AND CONFLICT RESOLUTION

Man is born into conflicts/frustration and the new born infant cries immediately after its birth. The uterine life is without any tensions, frustrations or conflicts for the foetus and the moment it comes to the world, it starts to face situations **(Pull Factors)** which necessitate many kinds of tensions/conflicts/frustrations. In order to escape from the tensions/conflicts and frustrations, man needs **Hope/Expectations.** Hope means "(i) the feeling that what is wanted can be had or that events will turn out for the best, (ii) to look forward to with desire and reasonable confidence. There is a usage i.e., hope against hope (to continue to it). Expectation—i.e., to look forward to; regard as likely to happen. Man needs **Hope/Expectations** for his onward journey particularly when he faces frustrations/conflicts/tensions. The **Spiritual Mind** has **Faith** and/or **Belief. Faith** in God/gods gives him an assurance that he will be blessed by the Almighty to get out of the frustrations/tensions/conflicts and he will get it by prayers—ardent prayers and continuous prayers. He makes offerings to please the Almighty with a hope that everything will be alright—a hope which he has. Create frustrations and frighten a man, give hope, show an invisible power and he gets out from his frustrations/conflicts/tensions by prayer. He has such an experience because he has a **Spiritual Mind** in him. The **Hope, Frustrations/Conflicts** and the **Spirit** have a triangular relationship.

So long as **Animality** works as an activating force in man, there will be frustrations and mental conflicts in people.

Instincts

1. *Escape*—A man wants to escape from a danger. He prays to God for help. He has the hope/expectation. Here **Faith** becomes necessary.
2. *Repulsion*—A man wants to get out of cancer which has affected his liver. He has frustrations and resorts to divine intervention. **Faith** is essential. He has **Hope/ Expectations** here.

3. *Food seeking*—A man cultivates vegetables and plants. They are destroyed owing to a wild wind. He does many things with a **Hope/Expectations** that he will get the benefit by them. **Belief** is needed to achieve the goal.
4. *Self-assertion*—A man fails continuously in university examinations. Still he studies with a **hope** that he will be successful at last. **Belief** in success becomes necessary.

Man has any number of frustrations and mental conflicts in life. He has been blessed with a number of defence mechanisms to escape from frustrations/mental conflicts. In order to have recourse to various escape mechanisms, he needs **Belief** or **Faith** or **Both.** Go to a church, a temple, a mosque, a pilgrim centre, a prayer hall and people come there with their frustrations, conflicts and problems. When they pray to God, they get tremendous amount of mental relief and feel thus satisfied. Man is an animal limited in time and space—and situations. He sees powers superior to him and ardent prayer or faith in spiritual beings is a sort of conflict resolution for him.

MORAL MIND[7] AND MENTAL PEACE

So long as **Animality** works in man as an activating force, he wants to reach his goal by any means--legal or illegal, moral or immoral, social or antisocial, ethical or otherwise. If he reaches the goal legally, morally without violating any laws, then he is mentally happy and at peace. Many a time, this is not possibe. In such situations, he wants to reach the goal by any means—fair or foul. Since, man has got such a mind, it is necessary to guide and control him *via* **Morality Mind** which contains all laws including the so named God given/made, divine, religious laws, rule, regulations, customs and traditions.

Instincts

1. *Acquisitiveness:* A man wants to become rich. Impossible

owning to many barriers. Frustration results, and mental conflicts seen. Resorts to illegal means—black marketing, hoarding, smuggling etc. Mental peace is distrubed. Hence, the **Morality/Ethics Mind** guides him and controls him for obtaining mental peace and happiness.

2. *Sex* : A man of 36 could not marry owing to several reasons. He understands that sexual satisfaction *via* legitimate marriage is difficult. He goes to a prostitute to have his sexual tension released. The **Morality-Ethics Mind** guides and controls him.

3. ***Combat (Pugnacity)***: A man wants to beat a man and he cannot do it legally or morally. He employs a *gunda* for the purpose. **Morality-Ethics** mind guides and controls him.

BELIEF AND SUPERSTITION

There is nothing called superstitious belief. Who decides the nature of **Belief**? If one is a real belief and the other is a superstitious belief, the question arises: "Who decides the true nature of the beliefs?" Both beliefs are invisible and the decision cannot be made by anybody. For example:

(1) This is a miracle from God, Almighty—is a *belief/faith(?).*
(2) This is a miracle from the Devil—is a *belief/faith (?).*
(3) This is not a miracle—this too is a *belief.*
(4) This is miracle because I found a Lizard looking at it. This is a *belief.*

Those which are enumerated under (1), (2), and (3) may be said to be superstitious beliefs/faiths (?) whereas the (4) will say that it is a belief. No body can say anything about the nature of a Belief/Faith (?) although (1), (2), (3) and (4) need a Belief/ Faith (?) 'to' live and survive. Recently, Pope Francis of the Catholic Church (2015) said that a good man need not necessarily be a believer (Having Faith) in God. At the same time, he needs to have a belief (not Faith in God) to live and survive. Rationalists, empiricists, humanists, atheists and so on have beliefs although they do not have **Faith** in God. For nobody can go forward without having beliefs in the invisible things. Tailhard De Chardin said that the evolution of mankind was to an Omega, the existence of which is not certain for many. Yet, the belief in Omega, according to him, becomes necessary for anyone. Yes, one's mother's identity is a reality whereas his father's is a **Belief** and in most of the time, the **Belief** is a reality. Today, there is a news in the media that a child of 3 years was sacrificed to please a deity to get treasure. They did so out of an animal instinct of Acquisitiveness (followed by an emotion of ownership) and they had the **Belief** (Not at all superstitious belief) that they would get the treasure. If they behaved out of their intelligence, they would not have done so. They had a **Spiritual Mind** overpowering the **Intelligence.**

PHYSICS AND METAPHYSICS[8]: BELIEF OR FAITH IN THE SUPERNATURAL

I studied **Ontology** for some time and Late Rev. Dr. Joseph Manickath told us about Physics and Metaphyics as under. When books were arranged in a library, they found some books which dealt with subjects other than **Physics.** In other words, the topics discussed were matters beyond the physical world and physics as conceived by them. They kept such books after the books in physics and called that section **"Metaphysics"**. He said further—

(1) There are many things in this universe and they cannot just be explained by the laws of physics or physical world.
(2) There are many things in this universe and they cannot be clearly understood by human intelligence.
(3) There are many things in this universe which are beyond the intelligence and they could be understood only by **Belief or/and Faith.**
(4) Man cannot live with his intelligence alone as he needs **Faith or/and Belief.** Faith in an invisible God or **"Beings"** in an invisible world is necessary for life on earth.

He was a Professor in a Catholic seminary giving training to aspirants to Catholic priesthood. They preached about God and worked as the Ministers of the Holy Church. In any case, I found them praying to God and in most of their prayers I could notice:

(1) An acceptance by the people that they are sinners, worthless people to stand before God, people of no value and who do not have any merits in them.
(2) A praise and glorification of God as Almighty who showers blessings in plenty on people, no matter, they are sinners, or saints. God is merciful, concerned, kind and sympathetic to people.
(3) Therefore, the prayer is to shower on the people, irrespective of their merits, the blessings so that their intentions are materalized. Everyone has a lot of frustrations, mental conflicts and anxieties which are solved, lessened or not increased by the Almighty. According to them, prayer is the only way to get God's blessings.
(4) Prayer is a panacea for all problems which humans have or suffer from.

In order to please the God, Almighty, people do all things or many things which they think may please ordinary people. Thus, one can see offerings and many rituals which make people happy, according to them, are pleasing and acceptable to God. The concept of a personal God who punished the people who committed wrong things also came into being.

GOD, GOD-MAN AND GODLY ATMOSPHERE

Once the concept of God or supernatural Being is accepted, then, it is necessary to have more and more **Pull Factors** to make the **Faith** stronger in the growing child. For this,

(1) The god-men appear with an attire/dress/vestments which create the feeligs of God or the presence of God.

Usually, they may have long beard, head-dress and special wearings of the dress creating divine feelings or heavenly thoughts.

(2) They appear in special and bright lights with illumination, perhaps with incence, fire, chantings etc. The sounds and the sound arrangements create a sort of euphoria in people that something supernatural is taking place at the platform where the god-man sits.

The prayers recited give people a special mental pleasure which they do not get otherwise. It is like the pleasure people have when they enjoy songs, listen to musical sounds, seeing a pleasant sight etc. Precisely therefore, the platform of the god-man will have all those visuals, auditory **Pull Factors** and people want them for the formation of an **Ego Factor** in them.

I was born and brought up in a Catholic family by ardent parents who had ardent **Faith in Jesus Christ** who was the saviour and the God of Christians. Every new born child in such a family is brought up in Catholic faith and, therefore, his **Ego Factor** is formed in the Catholic perception of God. A Hindu child is brought up in Hindu **Faith,** a Muslim in his **Faith,** a Jew in his **Faith** and a Sikh in his **Faith** and Jain in his **Faith** etc. Everyone has his own prayer centres. The tribals have their **Faith** in God and everyone develops an **Ego Factor** accordingly. This **Spirituality** along with **Morality/Ethics** and **Intelligence** works with the **Animality** of man.

What about the **Ego Factor** developing over the **Belief.** It has been said earlier that the **Foundation** of the **Ego** and the **Ego Factor** is put by the time a child reaches his puberty. Therefore, most of the people who are born and brought up in a particular **Faith** may continue to be in that **Faith** as it gives them special mental pleasure. Nevertheless, there will be some who may deviate from the **Faith** and they claim to have no faith in a personal God, but have only **Belief** in certain principles in life. Thus come the rationalists, humanists, atheists, materialists, Naxalites, and so on. They have no difficulty to accept a 'God', but they are not prepared to accept a personal God who is in heaven to bless the mortals on earth and punish the sinners when they reach heaven. If the concept of 'God' is identified with a Universal Power, they do admit such a 'God'. They do not accept prayers, religious services, pious rituals and rubrics etc. Accordingly, their **Ego** and the **Ego Factor** are formed.

Since, the foundation of **Faith** is laid down by the time a child has reached 13-14 years of age, it is not that easy to demolish such a foundation or base. Most of the people construct the superstructure on the **Foundation** and as such very many people have **Faith** in God as well as **Belief** in Eternal Principles/Universal power/a **Supernatural** power etc. This is the reason why the **Ego Factor** of many people is said to have built on a Spiritual Power, Moral Principles and Intellectual Convictions. Nevertheless, there may be extrimists in their **Faith** or/and **Belief.** Such people are found in religion, politics, humanism and humanitarianism etc. There are religious extrimists, fundamentalists, fanatics and terrorists. They create a lot of havoc and choas in the world. Likewise, there are socialists, Marxists, Maoists, Naxalites, advocates of Democracy and they too act in accordance to their **Belief** and/ or **Faith.**

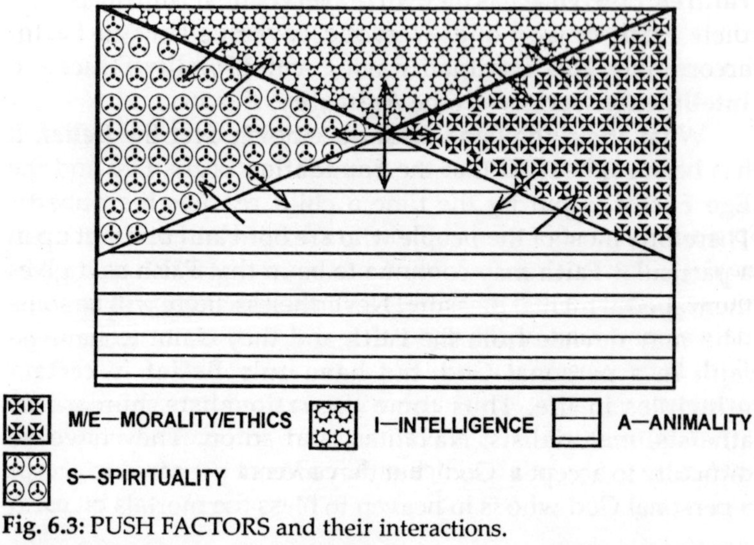

Fig. 6.3: PUSH FACTORS and their interactions.

My observation is that most of the people in the world have **Faith** in a god and **Belief** in a supernatural Power/Eternal Principles. Accordingly, the **Ego Factor** is formed with a spiritual mind in everyone. The Structure of the **Human Mind** with all **Push Factors** and their interaction are shown in Fig. 6.3.

The principle is that (1) There is interaction between—

(a) Intelligence and Spirituality and *vice versa.*
(b) Intelligence and Morality/Ethics and *vice versa.*
(c) Intelligence and Animality and *vice versa.*

(2) There is interaction between—

(a) Morality/Ethics and Spirituality and *vice versa.*
(b) Morality/Ethics and Animality and *vice versa.*

(3) There is interaction between—

(a) Spirituality and Animality and *vice versa.*

The interaction among the **Morality/Ethics, Spirituality, Intelligence** and **Animality** makes the **Push Factors** to interact with the **Pull Factors** to form the **Ego Factor** which, in my considered view, must be uprightly formed in the right direction if crimes are to be reduced in society.

INTERACTION BETWEEN INTELLIGENCE AND SPIRITUALITY AND VICE VERSA

Spirituality contains **Faith, Belief** or both. Faith and/or belief may not be blind as they have their basis in intelligence. Of course, there is a usage—blind faith, nevertheless, on a deeper analysis one may understand that the faith is not altogether blind. It may have some intellectual interpretation, historical backing or religious explanations transmitted from generations to generations. Hence, there exists an interaction between **Spirituality** and **Intelligence** or **Vice Versa.**

Illustration for Faith

1. The 'Faith' is that a particular disease was cured by God's intervention, i.e., a miracle. This 'Faith' is substantiated by a medical report stating that the cure was beyond medical capabilities. Here, the 'Faith' is mixed with 'Intelligence.'
2. The 'Intelligence' was that a particular satellite was launched after a lot of studies and calculations. But, the scientists make special *pujas* and prayers for achieving the sucess. For, they believe that there is a providence even in the falling of a sparrow. They have a number of instances to show that a lack of divine blessings resulted in the failure of many intellectual activities.

Hence, many people pray for godly interventions and blessings before they start doing any activity including intellectual work. Hence, everyone's intellectual **Ego (Mind)** has an element or portion of Faith, Belief or/and both mixed together.

Illustration for Belief

There may be rationalists, atheists, agnostics or empiricists and so on and they do not have any feeling about divine intervention or godly blessings. They have trust on intelligence and science. This is called Belief.

1. The 'Belief' is that the sun rounds the earth. People believed so because they found the sun in the east in the morning, above the head at noon and in the west in the evening. Although the scientific evidence (intelligence) was against the belief, people had a belief even against the scientific evidence.
2. There is a Cosmic law and what is it? Every act of a man will have an equal and opposite reaction. In other words, if a man does good things, he will get good

things back and conversely, if a man does bad things, he will get bad things back. What is the evidence or scientific explanation? No explanation, yet there is such a belief. There is nothing called 'Belief and Superstitious Belief.' Every body has beliefs and one's belief will be superstitious belief for another. Hence, intelligence or no intelligence, man has **Faith, Belief** or/and both in his **Ego.**

INTERACTION BETWEEN INTELLIGENCE AND MORALITY/ETHICS AND *VICE VERSA*

Morality/Ethics has or should have an intellectual base and precisely therefore, there is a constant interaction between Morality/Ethics and Intelligence. The intellectual basis, i.e., the norms which norm the norms—makes the moral/ethics norms meaningful.

Illustrations

1. *Euthanasia*—i.e., mercy killing is an immoral act. Why? Though it is an act of putting to death painlessly or allowing the sick to die, as by withholding extreme medical measure, a person or animal suffering from an incurable, especially a painful disease or condition, people think that it is an act of killing/murdering. Hence, not justifiable.
2. *Abortion*—the removal of an embryo or foetus from the uterus in order to end a pregnancy—is an immoral act as it is considered as a murder of an unborn child. Hence, there is the unsettling of the human mind when one resorts to abortions. The Ego Factor is formed out of push and pull factors which feels pain when it violates the law of the conscience—i.e., the moral laws.

INTERACTION BETWEEN INTELLIGENCE AND ANIMALITY AND *VICE VERSA*

Pugnacity (Combat) is an animal instinct and it interacts with intelligence. Man applies his intelligence whenever he attacks another and it is seen in the war or in any other combats.

Illustrations

1. The murder cases tried by the courts of law will show how intelligently people plan and execute their actions.
2. The acts of the mentally retarded (people having a low I.Q.) will show that their acts/activities—even attacks have more animality in them than intelligence. As they are suffering from a low I.Q., there is little or no interaction between animality and intelligence.
3. All animal instincts will have interactions with intelligence and the more the contents of intelligence, the better it will be.

INTERACTION BETWEEN MORALITY/ETHICS AND SPIRITUALITY AND *VICE VERSA*

Morality and spirituality are interrelated. Many of the moral principles are based on **Beliefs/Faiths** or both.

Illustration

1. "Look after the parents when they are old"—this is a moral principle which has a basis in Faith, Belief or both. In religious books, one sees God punishing those who neglect their parents (Faith) and in daily life, one sees many neglecting their old and infirm parents suffering from many ailments/mental depression (Belief).
2. "Never give false testimony before a court"—this is a moral principle which has a basis in faith (God's Ten Commandments) and in man's life one sees many hardships (sufferings)—psychological and physical when one does so (Belief).

INTERACTION BETWEEN MORALITY/ETHICS AND ANIMALITY AND *VICE VERSA*

Every instinctual behaviour should have a moral justification. Any instinctual (animal) behaviour without a moral justification is criminal (abnormal or immoral).

Illustration

1. Sexual acts (Animality) with a person married is fully justified morally. Otherwise, it is not as one may see in rape, adultery or unnatural sexual acts etc.
2. Acquisitiveness (Animality) expressed in dacoity, cheating etc. is morally not justified.

Hence, the **Ego Factor** is formed by mixing animality with morally justified/justifiable acts/omissions.

INTERACTION BETWEEN SPIRITUALITY AND ANIMALITY AND *VICE VERSA*

Any spiritual activity is acceptable if the animality is acceptable.

Illustration

1. Fasting is good and spirituality accepts it as something pleasing to God. But too much of fasting? It is abnormal and not acceptable.
2. Human sacrifice was considered to be a spiritual act in the past as something pleasing to God. But, now, it is considered as a crime as it is against the moral laws—or *Beliefs*.

Hence, what is the conclusion?. The **Ego Factor** formed as a result of the **Push** and **Pull Factors** will be a **Whole** functioning in unison. One cannot isolate intelligence from morality and *vice versa*. Likewise, he cannot isolate animality from spirituality and *vice versa* and so is the case with morality/ethics and spirituality/intelligence/animality. The **Ego Factor** is a mixture of all—intelligence, morality/ethics, spirituality and animality.

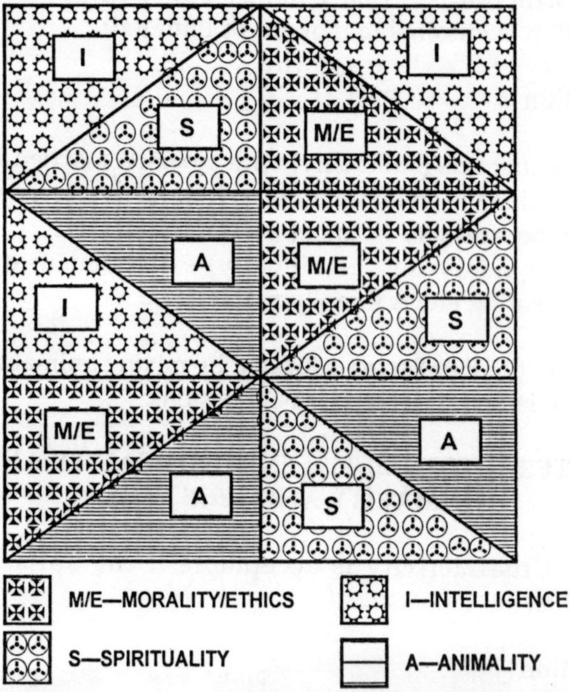

Fig. 6.4: Ego Factor AS A WHOLE (Thus, the Animality, Spirituality, Morality/Ethics and Intelligence work in unison as a **WHOLE** in an individual as his/her **EGO FACTOR**).

The intelligence, Animality, Spirituality, Morality/Ethics are not in watertight compartments. They are mixed together so much so that one cannot separate one from other/others. An individual means a person having his/her **Ego Factor** with **Intelligence, Morality/Ethics, Animality** and **Spirituality** grinded together to form a **whole.**

SPIRITUALITY, INDIVIDUAL, GROUP AND SOCIETY

My research observations are—

(1) All people have a **spiritual mind.**
(2) Most of them have **Faith** in God/gods and **Belief** in eternal principles/supernatural powers. Faith in God/gods depends upon the religion to which each one belongs. If they do not have a God/gods of an established religion (Christianity, Islam, Sikh, Hinduism etc.), then they will create a God/gods just like the tribals do.
(3) A few people are skeptical about a God/gods of a religion. Some are agnostics and some others are atheists. Compared to the theists, the number of the atheists may not be very large or huge. An atheist finds it difficult to live in a society, for every society is linked with some religion, religious practices and customs, traditions etc. Whatever may be the nature of such people, everybody has a **Belief** in a supernatural power/a universal power or eternal principles.

The conclusion is that man cannot live without a **spiritual mind** formed with **morality/ethics, intelligence and animality.**

What are my research observations of the **Spiritual Mind** of a group in a society? My observations are—

(1) People who have religious **faiths** form their own groups and they have a **group mind.** The priests, *sannyasis, pujaris,* god-men belong to such groups and such groups are seen in both sexes. They promote and propagate their **faith** to others and try to increase the number of faithful in a particular religion. If they become extrimists in their religious faith, gradually, they become fundamentalists, terrorists or fanatics and so on.
(2) Like those who have religous **faiths,** there are groups

which have **beliefs** in certain eternal principles, universal power etc. They do not accept or approve of a personal God/gods. Rationalists, empiricists, athiests, humanists (without religious God/gods) humanitarians (without God/gods), philanthropists and so on have a **Spiritual Mind** having only **beliefs.**

(3) One and the same group will have **faith** in a religious God/gods and **belief** in eternal principles, Cosmic Power, Universal Force etc.

(4) There is a likelihood that conflicts and disputes erupt among the various groups.

What about the research observation of a **society mind** as far as the spirituality is concerned? The observations are—

India is a secular nation. Nevertheless, there are nations in the world and they are theocratic. There are Islamic countries just like there are Christian countries. Former Christian countries have become Islamic during the course of history. Hence, the findings are—

(1) There are societies (nations) which have a **religious spiritual mind.** There too, there are people who do not have **faith** in a God/gods, neverthless have **belief** in a Cosmic Power/Universal Force or Eternal Principles.

(2) Society with purely materialist attitude cannot exist as man cannot live without spirituality. Some countries which attempted to be materialistic have died out in due course of time as they cannot exist and survive without spirituality. In a particular country, there was an Embassy where there were religious services. Though that country never permitted religious services in open places of worship, it was observed that the Embassy's prayer hall was full of faithful to participate in the religious services whenever conducted. In short, I have seen that there cannot be a society without spirituality and spiritual services. The pleasure and satisfaction

> which the spiritual services offer to people cannot be provided by anything else. Nevertheless, the spirituality of one group or denomination fights with the spirituality of another group/ denomination. Religious bigotry and communal fights do take in countries where different denominations and religions exist and survive. Conversion is seen and in some countries, one religious group attempts or makes attempts to convert people from one denomination to another, from one faith to another and thus fights and disputes are going on. In India, there is now a movement called **"Ghar Vapassi"** which means **"Going Back Home"** which means that those who were converted from one faith to another in the past are asked to go back to their earlier faiths and thus one sees fights, disputes and verbal wars on any attempts of conversion or reconversion. In the history of man, religious attacks and wars have been plenty and precisely therefore, I find a **Spiritual Mind** of the Society working with the **morality, intelligence** and **animality**. Thus, one hears about Christian morality, Hindu morality, Islam morality along with their special and specific rules/laws/customs and traditions.

When the **Spiritual Mind** overpowers a society, the society is expected to be law abiding, because God/Cosmic Power/ Universal Force/Eternal Principles are or should be at work. But, what is seen today is that the dominant **Spiritual Mind** of the society is overpowered by the **Animality** of the leadership in that society and as such they commit atrocities on the weaker sections of the society. This is the reason why countries which are secular in outlook give protection to the minorities as a Fundamental Right in their Constitution itself. There are courts established to protect the Constitutional Rights of the minority community. Nevertheless, the minority communities are victimized in the name of God/gods/religion/faith/belief and that becomes a burning issue in many parts of the world. Resultingly, extrimists, fundamentalists, fanatics and terrorists come into being and they create a hell in the name of religion. The next chapter deals more with the **Push** and **Pull Factors** and their interations.

Notes

1. Lucifer is a proud, rebellious archangel, identified with Satan, who fell from heaven.
2. In paganism, we see people observing polytheistic religion.
3. **BELIEF Means**—
    1. An opinion or conviction: a belief that the earth is flat.
    2. Confidence in the truth or existence of something not immediately, susceptible to rigorous proof: a statement unworthy of belief.
    3. Confidence, faith, trust: a child's belief in his parents.
    4. A religious tenet or tenets; religious creed or faith: to follow the Christian belief.
    5. Acceptance of or confidence in an alleged fact or body of facts as true or right without positive knowledge or proof. Belief is such acceptance in general: Belief in astrology.
4. **FAITH means**—
    1. Confidence or trust in a person or thing: Faith in another's ability.
    2. Belief that is not based on proof: He had faith that the hypothesis would be substantiated by fact.
    3. Belief in God or in the doctrines or teachings in religion.
    4. Belief in anything, as a code of ethics, standards of merit, etc. to be of the same faith with someone concerning honesty.
    5. A system of religious belief, the Christian faith, the Jewish faith.
    6. The obligation of loyalty or fidelity to a person, promise, engagement etc. Failure to appear would be breaking faith.
    7. The observance of this obligation: fidelity to one's promise, oath, allegiance, etc. He was the only one who proved his faith during our recent troubles.
    8. Christian Theology: the trust in God and in his promises as made through Christ and the Scriptures by which humans are justified or saved. (See, Random House Webster's *Unbridged Dictionary*, New York, 2001)
5. Aesthetics is a branch of philosophy dealing with such notions as the beautiful, the ugly, the sublime, the comic etc. as applicable to the fine arts, with a view to establishing the meaning and validity of

critical judgement concerning works of art and the principles underlying and justifying such judgements; study of the mind and emotions in relation to the sense of beauty. (Webster's)

6. The Exodus, the departure of the Israelites from Egypt under Moses; the second book of the Bible containing an account of exodus—i.e., departure.
7. Mind Means (in a human or other conscious being) the element, part, substance, or process that reasons, thinks, feels, wills perceives, judges etc. and in Psychology, it is the totality of conscious or unconscious mental processes and activities (Webster's). In Push-Pull-Ego Factor theory, it is the activating force or energy.
8. Metaphysics is a branch of philosophy that treats of first principles, includes ontology, cosmology and is intimately connected with epistemology. Metaphysical means concerned with abstract thoughts or subjects, as existence, causality or truth.

7
PUSH and PULL FACTORS: How do they Interact?

Demonology, as said earlier, speaks about the devils pulling people to commit sins and in Christianity, one finds Lucipher, the head of the hell with millions of devils pulling and pulling the weak, mortal and susceptible human beings to violate God's laws. Hinduism and other religions too accept the influence of evil spirits. The forces which pull people are nothing, but temptations[1] in fact. What demonology said during the pre-scientific period is what is repeated by victimologists now—during the twenty-first century. Victimologists speak about victims' role in inciting, tempting, attracting, allowing, encouraging, enticing etc. and they mean nothing, but the temptations given earlier by devils. Again there may be many be temptations offered by other forces, factors and situations. St. Thomas Aquinas (1225?-'74) a major theologian of the Catholic Church spoke about worldly temptations as the pulling forces to commit venial or mortal sins as the case might be. In order to get out of the temptations, Thomist approach was prayer—ardent prayer—continuous prayer to God. Classical School of Criminology said that there might be many pulling forces in society (environment) and they gave pleasure to people when they preferred to commit crimes by exercising their freedom of will. In Thomist as well as in classical school, one finds no much or any special importance or significance given to the pulling forces. The entire responsibility, in a way, for committing sins/crimes was put on the shoulders of the sinner/criminal alone and therefore the sinner/criminal was punished. When penal codes were written in the West, the law put the entire liability on the shoulders of the offenders and punished them without having any special considerations given to other factors compelling them to commit crimes. In religion too, the whole liability for committing sins was attributed to the sinners and they were awarded punishments accordingly. A fight with the devil by the weak mortal man was indeed unimaginable; yet he was punished. Though the geographical, topographical schools and thermal theories of crime causation approved/admitted the role of geography, topography, climate (hot or cold) as forces or pulling powers for the people to involve in the commission of crimes, they too ignored the role of the pulling environments and placed the entire responsiblity on the offenders. No one could blame them as they could not punish the compelling environmental forces for pulling people to commit crimes. William Bonger said that there could be no bank robbery if there was no bank in the locality. When statisticians started interpreting crimes and criminal activities, they found the socio-economic factors pulling people to commit crimes. Researches conducted in India unearthed the fact that good or bad harvests decided the nature and quantum of crimes. A good harvest meant no property crimes as people had money with them. All of them were talking about the traditional crimes which could be seen in the penal codes enacted during nineteenth and twentieth century. Now, the nature and type of crimes have changed and they include corporate crimes, white collar crimes, institutional crimes, JEL crimes, bureaucratic crimes, *Mafia*, international rackets, enforcement crimes, consensus crimes, communal crimes, religious bigotry, political crimes and thus it is just impossible to attribute any single or simple environmental or situational factor as the pulling force/power as the etiological factor in the commission of crimes. However, during the development of criminological thoughts from demonology, one sees some criminologists like William Bonger (as mentioned earlier) talking about criminal motivations and facilitating environments as the causes of crimes. William Bonger's approach, I consider, was a precursor or pre-runner to my **Push-Pull-Ego factor** theory of cirme causation. However, later researches ignored William Bonger's views as we notice that later researchers were more concerned with either the psychological factors or sociological factors of crime and criminal behaviour. The schools of psychology hitherto spoke of psychological forces as **Push Factors.** The schools of sociology spoke about enviornmental/situational, sociological factors as **Pull Factors.** It seems to me that none in psychological school or in sociological school said much about the interactions between the psychological and sociological factors to form an **Ego.** Perhaps, those who studied heredity and crime and those who studied environments and crimes combined together and said about the interactions between heredity and environments for the development of human personality. They stated that heredity and environments interact together to form the personality of a growing child. Nevertheless, there too, they did not say anything much about the formation of an **Ego Factor** in the personality as the result of the interactions.

Today, criminologists study about the **Ego Factor** in the commission of crimes. In law too, the emphasis on an **Ego Factor** of the offenders is seen and appreciated by the Legislature, Executive and Judiciary. Resultingly, considerations are given to the offenders when punishments are awarded. There are many explanations now seen in criminology to explain the formation of the **Ego Factor** as a result of the interations between the **Push** and **Pull Factors**. Earlier chapters have brought out the **Push Factors** as the mixture of **Animality + Morality/Ethics + Spirituality and Intelligence** combined together to form a **"Whole"** and that **"Whole"** interacts with the **Pull Factors** around an individual.

A man is born in a country geographically located somewhere in the world. He is brought up in a region with a language and culture (sub-culture) over which he has no controls. He is born into a family as the child of certain parents over whom he had no choice. He is living in a community of people—in an urban or semi-urban or rural area—in a religion—in a caste (subcaste)—in a race—in an ethnic group.

Doubtlessly, those factors do affect his ego development and personality formation. Politics, political parties, form of Government, education of parents, profession/occupation/job of the parents, size of the family, nature of the family structure, type of family, process in the family's financial conditions affect in very many ways the formation of his personality and conscience. Disoraganized family, broken family, home, emotions at home, siblings, joint or nuclear family, religion, faith in God/gods, value system etc. have decisive influence on the growing child. Psychologists assert that the personality is shaped by an interaction between hereditary potentials and enviornments. The environental forces are called **Pull Factors** in **Push-Pull Ego Factor theory** of crime causation.

DEVELOPMENT OF EGO IN AN INDIVIDUAL

How is the development? Earlier, it has been brought out the hereditary potentials, i.e., buds to become flowers during the passage of time. It has been proved that the **Ego** (i.e., Personality) is the product of heredity and environment. Heredity gives potential for development and environment provides facilities/opportunities for the development of the **Ego** (Personality) and the **Ego Factor** in an upright way in the right direction or otherwise. Erikson gives six stages of development. They are as under:

1. ***First stage*** (up to 1 year)—Formation of a basic sense of trust. ***Second stage*** (1-4 years): sense of autonomy is developed. ***Third and Fourth stages*** (4th year up to adolesence): a sense of initative is developed. ***Fifth stage*** (adolescence up to adulthood): a sense of identity is developed and lastly the ***Sixth stage*** (adulthood and upwards): a sense of intimacy is developed. Positive movement through these stages is, according to Erikson, the basis for normal personality **(EGO)** development (see, *Human Behaviour and Law Enforcement*).

   Sigmund Freud speaks about various stages for the

personality **(EGO)** development. They are the ***(i) Oral stage*** i.e., sucking stage and biting stage, ***(ii) Anal stage, (iii) Phallic stage, (iv) Latency stage, (v) Homosexual stage*** and finally ***(vi) Heterosexual stage.*** According to him, the basic values and attitudes in everyone are formed and strengthened by the time he/she reaches puberty. Freud talks about **Fixation, Oedipus, Electra complexes** etc., and there exist disputes and controversies about Freudian approaches. Nevertheless and doubtlessly, his approach to personality **(EGO)** development—has been recognized as important and worth-considering to understand abnormalities including criminal behaviour and their treatment.

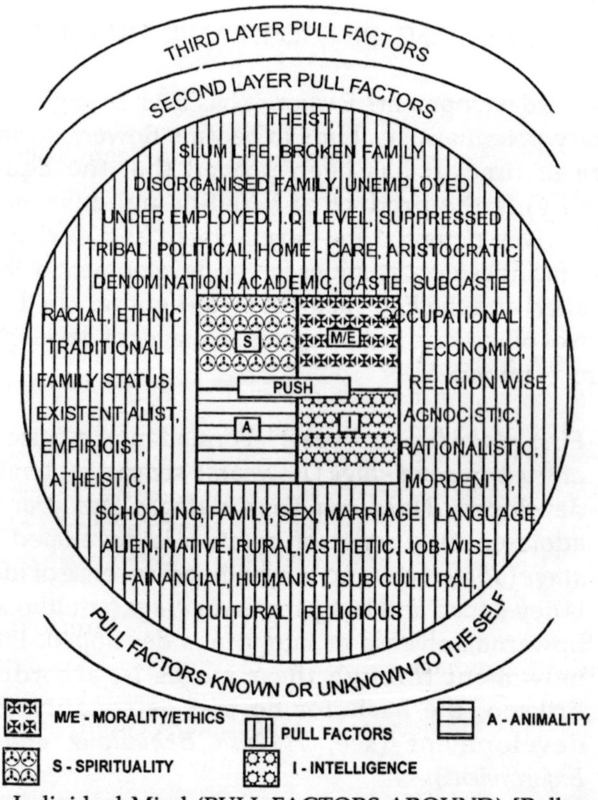

Fig. 7.1: Individual Mind (PULL FACTORS AROUND) [Pull and Push Factors shaping the Ego and the Ego factor of a developing child].

In Fig. 7.1, one sees **Push Factors** and **Pull Factors** for the formation of the **Ego** and the **Ego Factor.** As there is physical inheritance, there also take place social inheritance, religious and cultural inheritance. In social inheritance, one sees the inheritance of social, moral, and ethical values and in cultural inheritance, one observes the inheritance of the culture from generations to genrations. In religious inheritance, the religious (spiritual) values are inherited.

FORMATION OF A CRIMINAL EGO FACTOR

Inheritance—physical, social, religious and cultural—is important in the development of the **Ego** factor in a growing personality. In my researches, I have specially noticed the interaction between the **Push** and **Pull** Factors, to form and shape the **Ego** of an individual.

1. In criminal tribe community, it has been observed by me that the children born and brought up in that culture do not have any guilt feelings even when they commit crimes. They feel great and take pride in becoming criminals. A crime-doer is honoured by them. An ex-convict from a prison is preferred in marriage than a law abiding citizen.
2. I have seen that an association with people having special behavioural patterns make many to have their **Ego Factor** development in that direcion. Drug addicts, white collar criminals, those who involve in committing bureaucratic crimes, fanatics, fundamentalists, terrorists and extremists come under this category.

The interaction between **Push** and **Pull Factors** to form the **Ego** and the **Ego Factor** is shown the Fig. 7.2.

DEVELOPMENT OF EGO IN A GROUP

Individuals commit crimes and the penal codes speak mostly about such crimes and punishments. The sinner, the anti-social,

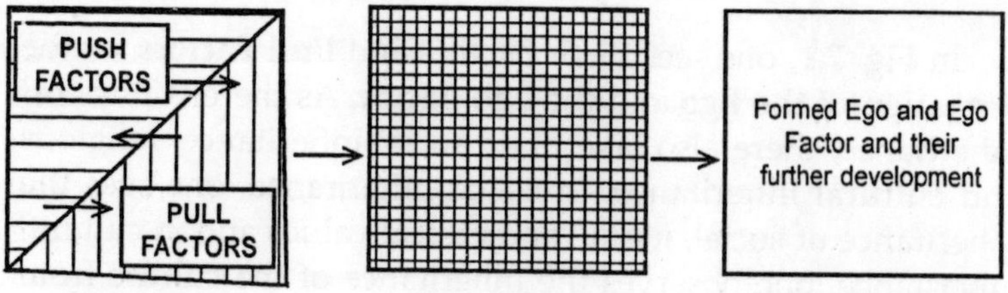

PUSH and PULL FACTORS Separately | Mixing together of Push and Pull Factors | Amalgamated Push and Pull Factors with Ego factor within the Ego/Personality

Heredity and environment in a neonate interact to form an Ego/Personality. In the Ego, the Push Factors—Intelligence, Morality/Ethics, Spirituality and Animality are seen.

Pull Factors—Environments, known and unknown in numerous numbers interact with push factors and the mixing is going on.

The Ego Factor after mixing of push and pull factors. One cannot separate push factors from pull factors when the ego factor is formed.

Fig. 7.2: Formation of Ego Factor after the mixing of Push and Pull Factors in the Ego/Personality.

the immoral, the criminal—all are individuals having an **Ego,** and the development has been discussed above. Now, crimes are committed by groups and they have no guilt feelings.

1. *White Collar Crimes:* They have **Animality + Morality/ Ethics + Spirituality + Intelligence.** They have an environment. The **Push** and **Pull Factors** form an **Ego** in them and it is called **Group Ego.** They speak the same thing in the same way. Examples: Naxalites, Maoists and so on.
2. *Bureaucratic Crimes:* Authority, Money power, Muscle power, no one to question, people's helplessness, people's acceptance etc. create a **Group Ego** that there is nothing wrong in committing bureaucratic crimes. Examples: corruption, bribery etc.
3. *Terrorists', Fundamentalists' Crimes:* Why the terrorists? Fundamentalists? in certain countries, the atmosphere, situations and environments justify their acts as virtues and consquently, no guilt feelings for

them. Rather, they have justifications and rationalizations. Examples: insurgents, terrorists and so on.

4. ***Organized Crimes:*** There is the demand and need. The ***Neta-Babu-Dalal-Dadah*** (leader-bureaucrats-middle man-*gundas*) philosophy/and approach make them feel that they can earn a lot of easy money without violating the laws applicable to individuals. Smuggling, pipe money etc. are of this kind.

Animality + Ethics/Morality + Spirituality + Intelligence (Push Factors) in a group have a Group Mind—with a **Group Ego**—formed owing to the interaction with enviornmental forces and factors—**Pull Factors.**

The white collar criminals in a particular sphere (say, medicine, insurance, chartered accountancy, law etc.) form a particular **Ego** for each one's group. Likewise, the Bureaucrats (say, police, sale tax, excise, income tax, law enforcement, judiciary etc.) form each one's **Group Ego** just like the terrorists on various reasons form each one's **Group Ego.**

Each Group gets favourable **Pull Factors** from each one's **Ego.** For example, the helplessness of the general public, dearth of effective laws, unholy nexus between the group, criminals and the adminisitration, money power, muscle power etc. make them to involve in the commission of crimes. The corporate crimes are of this category and everyone involved in the commission of these crimes has no guilt feelings, rather feels proud of their group crimes. Nobody can be caught as individual offenders as the crime has only a corporate *mens rea* and corporate criminal liability. Those who come to the group have a policy of *coming and going* and precisely therefore criminal liability cannot be fixed on a single individual.

From my researches, I take note of the fact that there exists a **group mind** and a group **Ego Factor.** I do not exempt any group from the commission of crimes. A society is formed out of many groups and sub-groups. MacIver's definition of society makes it very clear that there cannot be a society without groups and sub-groups. In my observations, I find every group/

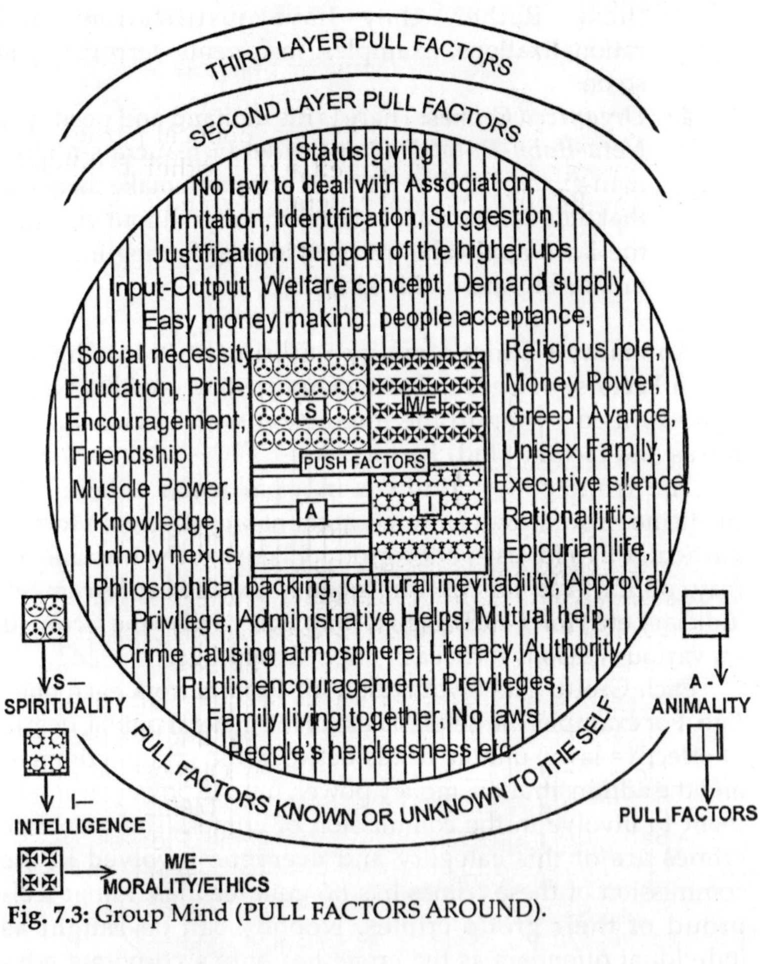

Fig. 7.3: Group Mind (PULL FACTORS AROUND).

sub-group in any society commits crimes which are for their advantage. Such groups are found on the basis of religion, denomination, caste, sub-caste, finance, profession, occupation, art, culture, region, sub-region, education, sex, age and what not? Every group has **Pull Factors** as well as **Push Factors.** An interaction between the **Push** and **Pull Factors** in each group makes them to have an **Ego Factor.** This **group-mind** and the subsequent **Ego Factor** become a cause of crimes.

Illustration

1. Crimes by labour unions, by business men, by *Mafia,* by professionals, by school children and so on.
2. Crimes by communal groups, political parties, rural people, corporates, media and other publishers, producers of cultural programmes and films etc.

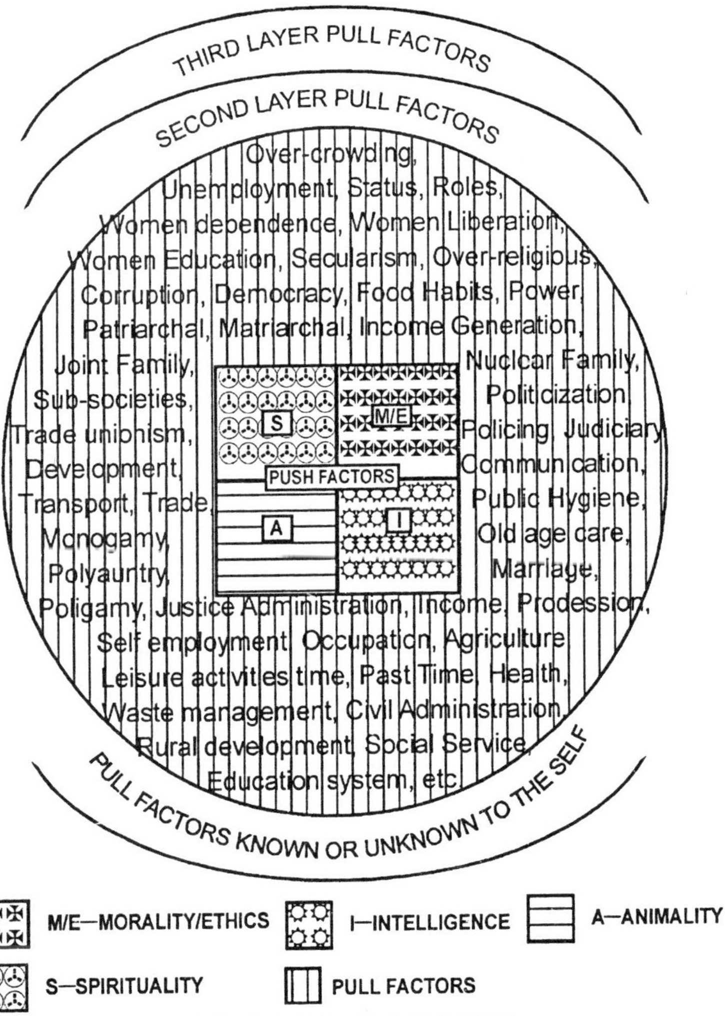

Fig. 7.4: Society Mind (PULL FACTORS AROUND).

The groups commit crimes for the benefits of the group/ group members. They do not claim to have a group *mens rea* and therefore fixing criminal liability over the group is indeed difficult in the existing justice system. The penal laws are individual based and not group based and the crimes the Penal Codes define can be/are committed by individuals with an **individual mind and Ego factor.** Here, in group crimes, the crimes are committed by the **Group Mind** and **Group Ego Factor.** As such punishing the offenders by applying the principles to fix individual liability cannot be applied. Hence, they escape punishments and cases are acquitted by the courts after trials.

Just like the **Individual Mind** with an **Ego Factor, Group Mind** with an **Ego Factor,** there exist a **Society Mind** and an **Ego Factor.** Because of such a mind and **Ego Factor,** such societies commit crimes on people other than theirs. Some of our neighbouring countries have a **Society** and **Ego Factor.** Such countries do a lot of harm to India including wars, encrochment of Indian land and they kill the people. Same thing is seen in several parts of the world. What actions can be taken against war crimes? Of course, there are some international treaties and nothing more.

Coming to a particular country, there will be societies formed on the basis of regionalism, language, religion etc. The **"sons of the soil"** approach and the crimes which the people adhering to such a philosophy may commit are owing to the **Society Mind** and **Ego Factor.** Some societies want to expel foreigners and they commit atrocities against them. Male society becomes hostile to female society, patriarchy becomes enimical to matriarchy and crimes are committed. Apartheid and the racial crimes are the result of the **Society Mind** and **Ego Factor.** Sometimes, terrorists' activities can be resulted.

Individuals exposed to particular **Pull Factors** have interactions with their **Push Factors** to form a **Group Mind** resulting in an **Ego.** The Individuals react as a **Group** and likewise the people living in a particular society develop a **Society Mind** and an **Ego Factor** accordingly.

DUCKLING APPROACH

There was a time some criminologists argued that people learn to commit crimes just like ducklings start swimming in water. It was Gabriel Tarde who said that imitation was the process through which people learnt to commit crimes. Later, some social psychologists added identification, suggestion etc. to imitation. Tardian imitation was accepted for some time as it was found to be a good explanation of criminal etiology. Later his approach was rejected as some who lived in the same society or exposed to the same social situations did not learn to commit crimes.

Edwin H. Sutherland came up with his Differential Association theory of crime causation and he also said about learning as a process by which people learnt the mechanics and techniques of committing crimes. I have my reasoned objections to accept Sutherland's Differential Association theory as no one learnt to commit the crimes just like that. There takes place some interactions between the individual and the environments. This is what is said by sub-cultural theories. In culture conflict theory, it is accepted that crimes are the results of culture conflicts and culture of one person has conflicts with the culture of another person. Again, the culture of one society conflicts with the culture of another society. The sub-cultural theories too accepted the samething in a different way. Children/people in one sub-culture go to another sub-culture and they commit crimes. Cultural lag theories too subscribed to the same process of interaction between the people and the culture. Material culture conflicts with the non-material culture and all such processes and learnings, interactions with the people and the social situations around them are seen. Hence, I have formulated my own approach to explain the interation and it is called the **grinder approach.**

GRINDER APPROACH

Every individual has **Push Factors** and every society has **Pull Factors.** They are put together to a **Grinder** and a mixture is obtained. This **Mixture** is called the **Ego** and the **Ego Factor** of an individual. If one adds colour to the grinder when grinding is going on, then the **Mixture** will have a special colouring. For example, a new born child is given a conducive family atmosphere, then his **Ego** and the **Ego Factor** will have that as a projected/dominating content. Take another example. If a group (a race or a caste) is taken, then the status of the race/caste will affect the **Mixture** to form the **Ego** and the **Ego Factor** of the group. The same is applicable for a **Society** as a whole. Take a society (religion, region, culture) and the **Mixture** will have the **Ego Factor** of the society.

The coloured **Grinder Mixture** with special **Ego** and specific **Ego Factor** will activate a person/group/society when he/they interact with others/situations. This interaction is explained by me with the help of **Piston Approach.**

PISTON APPROACH

Borrowing Locard's Principle of Exchange from the science of investigation, i.e., *when two things come into contact, there is an exchange of material. The more the contact, the more will be the exchange*—we may say that during the process of grinding, there is an exchange of **Push** and **Pull Factors.** This exchange when mixed will have special colours and the product, i.e., the **Ego** and the **Ego Factor** will be unique proving once again the Quatlet's Law of Individuality i.e., *"Nothing created by God or made by man will be identical."* Hence, every **Ego** and the **Ego Factor** will be unique and it is this **Ego** and the **Ego Factor** which are activated when a crime is committed or when a law is abided by. This activation force is like **Pistoning.** The more the *pistoning* takes place, the more will be the activation. The next chapter is about the process of activation when crimes are committed.

(1) The **push factors** and **pull factors** are seen separately.
(2) Through the **grinder process,** a **mixture** of **push** and **pull factors** is made.
(3) **Colouring** is seen in every individual depending upon

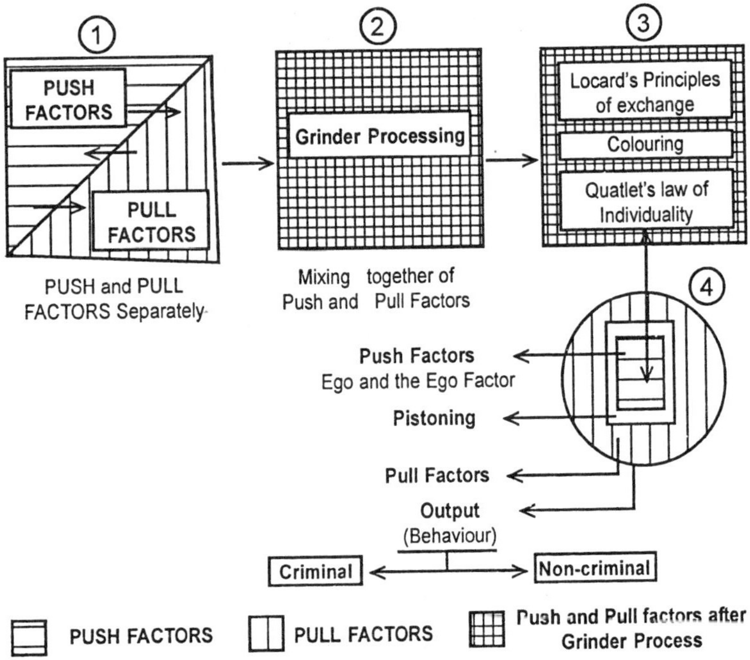

Fig. 7.5: Grinding & Pistoning.

the interaction between **Push** and **Pull** Factors. This is a mixture formed basing on **Locard's Principle of Exchange** and **Quatlet's Law of Individuality**. The **Mixture** formed is individualistic and it is the **Ego** and the **Ego Factor.**

(4) **Ego** and the **Ego factor** are in the **piston** and **pistoning** goes on in the situations (**pull factors**) provided. There is ardent interaction and the **output** will be either a **criminal behaviour** or a **non-criminal behaviour.**

This process is seen not only among the individuals, but also in groups and in societies. Hence, this will explain the causative factors of not only individual crimes, but also group and society's crimes. Thus, individual crimes like murder, rape, kidnapping as well as group crimes like corporate crimes, *Mafia*, organized racketeering, nexus crimes, consensus crimes,

JEL crimes etc. and society crimes like wars, racial crimes, communal crimes etc., are explained.

Examples

A. A girl born and brought up in a brothel does not become a prostitute. Why? When the girl is subjected to a process-wise analysis, what happens? In process (1) There are **push factors** and **pull factors.** In process (2) i.e., during the **grinder process**, a mixture is formed. In process (3) i.e., there is colouring and the **Ego** and the **Ego factor** in the **piston** are not having any crime-instincts dominating. Hence, in process (4) i.e., the anti-crime-instinct is very powerful and dominates the situation. She does not become a prostitute.

B. A boy born and brought up in a priestly home becomes a robber when he is just 22 years of age. Why? The crime-instinct is so potent in the **ego** and the **ego factor** and they dominate the situation.

C. A crime syndicate involved in smuggling make a lot of wealth within two years. The **group mind** and the crime-instinct in the **Group Ego Factor** have really exerted a domineering impact on the situation.

D. A society consisted of high caste people never allows members of low caste to mix and mingle with their children. Why to speak of such a social isolation? Martin Luther King in U.S.A. exhorted his people to fight against the discrimination of people on the basis of colour. No doubt, the criminal instinct was very powerful among the blacks who were suppressed by the white.

FORMATION OF THE EGO FACTOR IN AN UPRIGHT WAY IN THE RIGHT DIRECTION

Criminologists speak about the formation of the **ego** and the **ego factor** in an upright way in the right direction. What is the upright way? How can the **ego** be formed uprightly? What is the right direction? All these areas come under discussion when control of crime or reduction of crime is discussed. Criminologically speaking, a therapy in the psyche of the individuals, in the psyche of the group, in the psyche of the society becomes essential for the purpose. Sociologically speaking, a therapy, i.e., sociotherapy—is required to make the **pull factors** acceptable and desirable.

Both animals and men have instincts and they activate them to behave. Psychologists have so far identified 14 animal instincts and they say that the instincts can be shaped, modelled or developed in a particular direction. This is possible in people whereas it is not that easy in animals, birds, reptiles or fishes. Of course, certain animals can be tamed or trained to behave in a particular way to a limited extent. Elephants, dogs, cats, monkeys, dolphins, doves, parrots, eagles etc. are given training and one may see such trained animals, birds, fishes etc. in zoos, circus and in daily life. Certain birds are trained to behave in a particular way. Dolphin like fishes are trained. However, man can be trained and this is what is called socialization by sociologists and formation of conscience by psychologists, superego formation by Freudian Psychoanalysts, Parent-ego formation by Transactional Analysts, **moral mind** by moralists and so on.

Can the instinctual potencies in man be uprightly formed in the right direction? Right direction is decided by **morality/ ethics. Morality/Ethics** may mean the best and acceptable ways of behaviour for the best interest of the self and the society. This is decided by the laws, rules, regulations, traditions, customs etc. which control or ought to control human instincts. Human intelligence has a major role in controlling the human instincts and in developing them in the right direction. Intelligence has got the capacity to analyse everything critically and it helps a lot to form the human conscience uprightly in the right direction. Added to it, the **morality/ethics** and **spirituality** too help the formation of the human conscience in the right way or wrong way.

How is the human instinct developed in the wrong direction? This can be effected by providing wrong or criminal enviornments— **pull factors.** Any human instinct up to a certain extent/level is good and needed. Beyond that level, it is not needed rather is criminal or vulgar.

Illustration

Acquisitiveness (accompanying emotion is feeling of ownership) is an instinct. How much one should have or one needs? This is to be decided by the self. If the self is unable to decide it, then the society in its corporate capacity will decide it. Income Tax laws will be enacted. Everyone is legally bound to pay the Income tax. Out of his greed for money, he does not pay Income Tax. He manipulates the account and thereby he is violating the Income-Tax laws. The violation can be by an individual, institution or groups. If it is done by an institution, it becomes a corporate crime. It can be by a society and thus the crime is committed.

The instinct of acquisitiveness may make some people to commit theft, robbery, dacoity, misappropriation of property. It means that the instinct goes beyond the limits and thus violates the penal laws. Here too, the violations can be committed by institutions or groups. Then, the crime will be known by other names such as white collar crimes, commission or consultation (both are corruption) money, insurance frauds, charity frauds, offerings to God, donations to humanitarian works etc. Here, one sees the instinct of acquisitiveness going beyond the permissible limits. There may not be any penal laws to catch them and brand them as criminals. Here come the moral laws—i.e., the law of the conscience. The violation is linked with guilt feelings. Again, there are the spiritual laws (divine laws by religion) which make such acts as sins and the punishment is given after death. People speak about Cosmic Laws, Nature's Laws etc. to punish them on earth.

In order that the instincts are not developed in the wrong direction, it is necessary to inculcate **values** in them and it is done *via* moral/ethical laws, divine or religious laws, penal or State made laws, social, cultural or insitutional laws assisted by intelligence. The responsibility is taken—is to be taken by the mother, parents, family, community, neighbourhood, schools, teachers, friends, media, culture, cultural programmes, religions, instiutions, character building agencies, political parties, administration, police, justice system, welfare activities, social work, educational system, *"...sophies"*, *"....isms"*, and *".....ologies"*, humanitarian ideas, human rights promotions, protection methods of the weaker and handicapped sections of the society, women's empowerment and thus one can enumerate one thousand and one environmental—**pull factors**—factors for the purpose. In short, one may write the development of instincts as under.

S = Situations **(all pull factors)**
I-Instincts **(with other push factors)**

The instincts along with other push factors fight with the situations or interact with the situations. In other words.

(1) **Pull Factors ÷ Push Factors**
(2) **Pull Factors × Push Factors**

In (1) i.e., $\dfrac{\textbf{Pull Factors}}{\textbf{Push Factors}} \div$

and if it is above 1, i.e., the nominator more powerful than the denominator, then the **animal instincts + spirituality + morality/ethics + intelligence** are overpowered by the situation **(pull factors)**. In other words, there will not be an excess of push powers. The net result is that there will not a crime then. If the **pull factors** are weak, a crime will be the result.

In (2) i.e., **Pull Factors × Push Factors,** the product will be very powerful. This is good or bad meaning thereby one may be a law abiding or law violating as the case may be.

Again in (1) i.e., $\dfrac{\textbf{Pull Factors}}{\textbf{Push Factors}} \div$

the denominator will have a higher value than the nominator. In that case, the **animal instincts + spirituality + morality/**

ethics + intelligence overpower the situation. If push factors have gone beyond the permissible limit, then a violation of crime is the net result.

Hence, **formation** of the **ego factor** in an upright way in the right direction means—

(1) Make the **animal instincts + spirituality + morality/ ethics + intelligence (push factors)** to remain within the permissible limit. In other words, the **push factors** should obey the moral, penal, social, cultural, ethical, institutional laws.
(2) Make the situations **(pull factors)** very law abiding. In other words, provide a conducive atmosphere in the family, community and society for the development of instincts in the best way—up to the permissible limit.

This is the reason why criminologists advise for the creation of as many law abiding conditions and as much conducive atmosphere for the development of values in people and in society—a society with values ensures a society with law abiding people.

Note

1. Tempt means, "to entice or allure to do something often regarded, as unwise, wrong or immoral and here" it is sin/crime/vice etc.

8
Push-Pull Interaction and Ego Factor

That was a Sunday evening. I went to the down town and I found a man with a dagger chasing another. Yes, I was just stuck and then I found a police party on their patrol duty coming. Immediately, the man with the dagger vanished into the thin air. How could that happen in the way I saw it? **Push-pull-ego factor** theory has an answer to it. The theory says :

(1) Man has **push factors,** i.e., (a) **Animality,** (b) **Morality/ Ethics,** (c) **Spirituality,** and (d) **Intelligence.** Animality has instincts and the instincts are of many types. One of the instincts is **pugnacity** (Combat) with an accompanying emotion called **anger.** With **pugnacity,** which was the dominating instinct in him at that time, he was running with a dagger after a man at a higher speed [**escape** was the instinct in the man found fleeing away from the aggressor].

(2) As soon as the aggressor saw the police party, he transferred his animal instinct to **morality/ethics, spirituality** and **intelligence sphere** so much so that he vanished into the thin air.

What does it mean? It means—

(1) Man has the capacity to transfer the energy from

the **instinctual sphere** to another non-instinctual **sphere** or to the whole sphere consisting of all **push factors.**

(2) A transfer from the **instinctual sphere** to another non-instinctual sphere or to the whole sphere consisting of all **push factors** will result a totally different behaviour.

GROUP MIND, PUSH FACTORS AND EGO FACTOR

One religion in India has two divisions—groups—sects or denominations. They were inimical to each other. Both of them had only one prayer center and one cemetery where they buried the dead belonging to both denominations.

There was a Court Order which said that they could conduct prayer services at two different times fixed by the Court as under—

> *GROUP-A* should conduct their prayer service from 9 a.m. to 11 a.m. and *GROUP-B* should have it from 11.15 a.m. to 12.15 p.m. on a particular Sunday.

Accordingly, *GROUP A* had their prayers at the fixed time. They finished their prayers at 11 a.m. when they found the dead body of a faithful belonging to *GROUP A* being carried to the cemetery by the members of *GROUP A.* As their prayer time was over by 11 a.m., the members of *GROUP B* objected to the burial at the time allotted to them—i.e., after 11 a.m. There were heated verbal attacks among the members of both groups—*GROUP A* wanted to bury the dead body and *GROUP B* refused to permit it. There was a real law and order problem. Anything could take place.

Hearing the news, the police party arrived with the religious leaders of both groups and seeing the police party with religious leaders, peace was re-established. The ***group mind*** and the **ego factor** became law abiding. What does it mean? It means :

(1) *A Group* has the capacity to transfer the **group instinct** from the animal instinctual sphere of the ***group mind*** to another non-instinctual sphere or to the whole sphere consisting of all **push factors** of the **groups.**

(2) A transfer from the animal instinctual sphere (of the **group**) to another non-instinctual sphere of the group or to the whole sphere consisting of all **push factors** will result a totally different behaviour.

The **group mind** and the **group pull factors** and the **group ego factors** behave exactly like the individuals who behave in similar situations.

SOCIETY MIND, PUSH FACTORS AND EGO FACTOR

I have researched into the precipitating[1] and predisposing[2] causes of communal riots in Kerala from 1962 onwards. I have found that simple things get magnified—a mountain is made from a mole-hill—in many occasions. I have noticed that the **society mind** of one religion, the **society push factors** and the **society ego factor** of a particular religion has been contaminated with animal **instincts**—especially the instincts of **pugnacity, self-assertion, repulsion and escape.** Whenever or wherever riots erupt, the ruling Governments, political parties, religious leaders, police, publicmen, civic-minded people, peace loving men, moralists, spiritualists—all work together by negotiations and discussions to have a transfer from one sphere to another or to the whole sphere consisting of all **push factors** to re-establish peace in society. Resultingly, the **society ego factor** gets changed and overpowers the **pull factors** which are found to be operative and very operative.

Here too, the **society mind,** the **society pull factors** and **society ego factors** behave exactly like the individuals or groups who or which behave in similar situations.

In Fig. 8.1, we see the **animality sphere** overpowering the other spheres among the **push factors**—namely, the

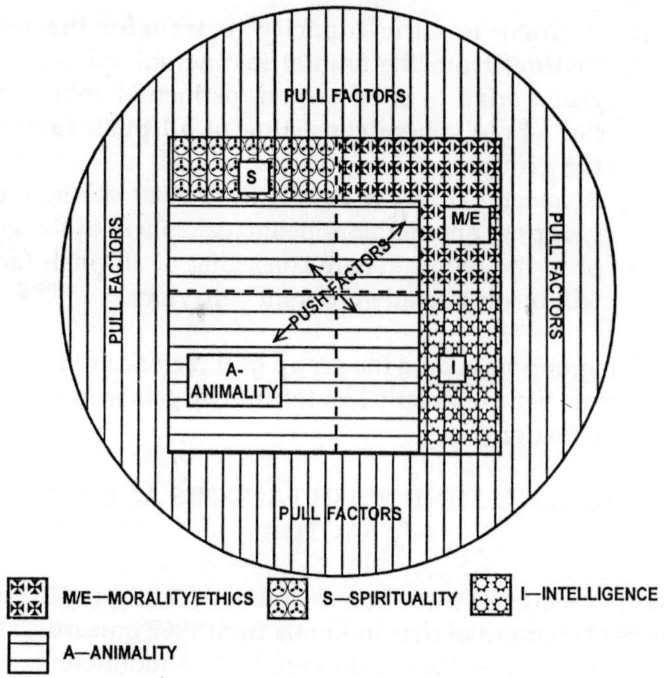

Fig. 8.1: Animality overpowering the Push Factors to form the Ego Factor.

spirituality, morality/ethics, intelligence. Though all the **push factors** interact with the **pull factors,** it is the **animality sphere** that overpowers. The **animality sphere** contains all instincts and it is necessary to identify the specific/special instinct/s which is/are found operative. For example—

(1) A man desires to become rich one day too soon. The instinct—i.e., self-assertion (feeling of superiority is the accompanying emotion) activates him. Precisely therefore, it overpowers the other instincts and the **animality sphere** devours all other spheres (morality/ ethics, spirituality and intelligence) and interacts with the **pull factors** to such an extent that it overpowers the **pull factors.** Hence, he commits theft or involves himslef to any criminal activity with economic motives.

If he behaves from the permissible limits of animality, then he does not become a crime-doer.

(2) Overpowered by the instinct of **sex** (lust is the accompanying emotion), rape is committed. The **ego factor** interacted with **pull factors** [by fight (÷) or by co-operation (×)] and won over the **pull factors.**

(3) Overpowered by the insitincts of **food seeking** (accompanying emotion is appetite) and **repulsion** (accompanying emotion is disgust), a group committed food riot. More than one insitncts may work on individuals or groups. Sometimes, the instincts may be four or five. Because, several members constitute the group.

(4) Overpowered by the instincts of **escape** (fear is the accompanying emotion), **pugnacity** (anger is the accompanying emotion), **appeal** (distress is the emotion accompanying), **repulsion** (disgust is the emotion), a society may involve in the commission of arson, mass destruction, murder, sexual assaults, etc. This is what is seen in a violent mob agitating against the **pull factors** operating in the society. This is what is happening in aggressive mobs (hostile mob), panicky mobs (fear stricken or escape mobs), acquisitive mobs etc. The members of the mob have different emotions and as such, they exhibit intense emotions and some times, they behave irrationally. They have crisis and the sense of crisis benumbs their brain so much so that other pull factors (morality/ethics, spirituality and intelligence). In fact, the mind refuses to function properly. The survival instinct is so powerful in the members of the society and as such they do not have any concern/consideration for others.

(5) An individual overpowered by the instincts of **curiosity** (wonder is the accompanying emotion), he may commit crimes which cause wonder. In gambling one may see this instinct. In drug addiction, curiosity works as a powerful instinct and it is interacted by association with others having similar habits of drugs. In some such

cases, an individual, being overpowered by the instinct of **gregariousness** (accompanying emotion is feeling of loneliness), may become a drug addict, a professional gambler or an alcoholic, etc.

(6) Groups like *Mafia,* Nexus criminals, Enforcement criminals, JEL criminals, Bureaucratic criminals, Corruption and Commission agents, White collar criminals, Smugglers, groups involved in investment frauds, charity frauds, devotion rackets, tender flesh trades—all commit crimes owing to excess of instinctual forces/factors. Instincts like **self-assertion** (feeling of superiority), **constructiveness** (feeling of creativeness), **acquisitiveness** (feeling of ownership) etc. will overpower the other **push factors** (morality/ ethics, spirituality etc.) to make economic benefits and fortune with the help of **intelligence.** Intelligence plays a good role in the expression of the instinctual forces. Morality/ethics and spirituality will have little or no role when the groups involve in the commission of economic crimes.

Push-pull-ego factor theory is applied not only to explain the criminal activities, but also to explain non-criminal activities. It may be reiterated that every instinct is necessary for activation. The instinctual expression becomes criminal if and only if or when and only when the expression goes beyond a level or crosses the threshold to criminality. An act/omission becomes criminal when the society in its corporate capacity says so.

SPIRITUALITY OVERPOWERING PUSH-PULL FACTORS

Fig. 8.2 depicts a situation in which the **spirituality sphere** overpowers other **push factors (animality, morality/ethics, intelligence).** It may be said again that the spirituality has either **faith or belief** and in certain people both **faith or belief** may be seen. They believe in the personal God/gods, Cosmic Power, Absolute Principles, Universal Force etc. and they are spiritual

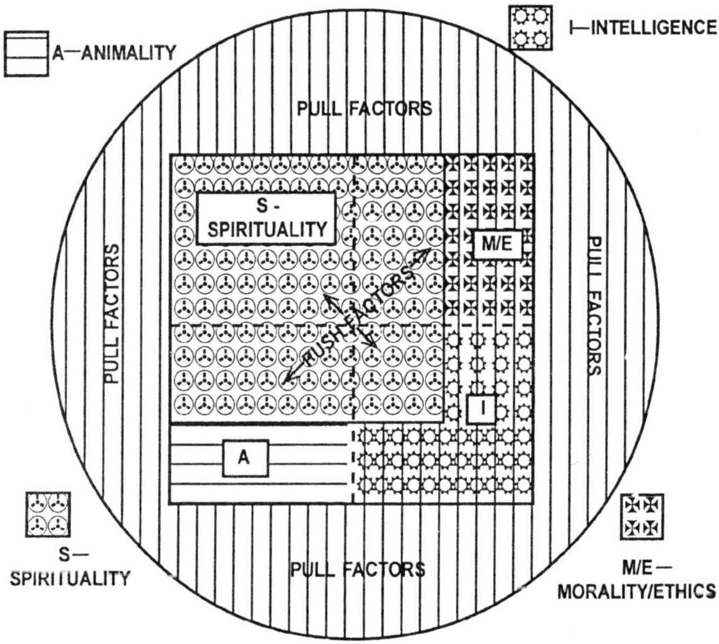

Fig. 8.2: Spirituality overpowering the Push Factors to form the Ego Factor.

in nature. Some have **blind faith** while some may not have a blind faith. Again, some will have unquestionable **belief** while others do not have such a belief. In any case, the Faith, Belief or Both will overpower the **push factors** in human mind. Those people overpowered by **spirituality** may or may not commit crimes, but more often than not, will become victims of crime. They will be misused, exploited, abused or victimized by those who have an excess of animal instincts in them. How?

Examples

1. An astrologer made huge amount of money by his predictions. An income tax raid proved that he amassed wealth by his spiritual tricks and dubious ways which were criminal in nature and sense.

What do you see here? Just like drug addiction, some people have prayer addiction, piety addiction, astrologer addiction. This is owing to an excessive or overpowering effect of **"spirituality" (?)** in them. The **'spirituality' (?)** overpowers the **morality/ethics** and **intelligence** in them. Such people are misused/abused by those people who claim to be the god-men.

Uncertainties are plenty in a man's life. A man has anxieties, frustrations, mental conflicts, disappointments, diseases and a lot of other problems. They want to get out of them and therefore everyone should have **"hope".** Actually, this hope is provided by **belief, faith** or both in people. A belief in a Cosmic Power/Universal Force/Eternal or Absolute Principal becomes essential for the survival of the people with a **hope** and some times, with a **hope** without **hope.** Instead of such Power/Force, some people have **faith** in the God/gods/godesses and in some instances, there may be personal or human gods. In any case a man cannot live and survive without this **"spiritual push factors"** in his mind. Just now, I read in **facebook :** "A man cannot survive if he has no belief in his own ability". O.K. I have personally conducted researches in this area and am convinced about the need for **belief, faith** or both for people to live and survive. It is needed for the **groups, society, nation, world** to proceed further. This **spiritual sphere—push factor** is misused/abused by vested interests in many ways. Nevertheless, any belief or faith, however strong it is, cannot be a substitute for a fact.

Spiritualists, Spiritual men, *Pujaris,* Prayer men, Evangelists, *Sadhus, Sannyasis,* Human gods, *Avatars* or Incarnates, Religious men, Scripture workers, Pulpit speakers, people who call spirits/ghosts, devil worshippers, those who perform black-magics, *mantravada, kudotram, chatenseva,* tribal priests, ritual performers and thus one sees hundreds and hundreds of people surviving because of the existence of the **spiritual sphere** in human mind and its powerful **"push factor"** effects. I have interviewed many of these "spiritual men" and I have collected a lot of research data that many of them work for earning an income from their so named "services". They call their work as **"spiritual service"** and some of them were candid enough to speak out that theirs were "services with a hook" —the hook being amassment of wealth. I have not seen or heard any "spiritual man" who died of poverty, but have seen/heard many who died out of affluence. They amass wealth and fortune under the colour of spirituality or under the cover of divine intervention. Not only individuals but also groups and the society involve in many nefarious activities under the colour of their spiritual garb or under the cover of gods' interference. If there are no crimes, no policemen will survive. For the survival of the policeman, crimes are needed. If they do not see crimes, they will create crimes for their survival. Likewise if there are no gods/religions, these *pujaris* and priests cannot survive. Hence, if there exist no gods, they will create them for their existence and survival. For, the policeman knows that there is **animality** in people as a **push factor** just like the *pujaris* and priests know that there is **spirituality** as a **push factor** in all people.

CRIMES OF SPIRITUALITY

I spoke of uncertainties in people and the need for assurance. The crimes are : insurance frauds, medical treatments frauds, mediclaims' hidden agenda, white collar crimes committed by religious societies, special divine blessings, compaigns, retreat centres, relics—sales, special prayer services, divine pilgrimages—all of them give assurance and people's "Spirituality Push Factor" is exploited here more than other spheres of the human mind.

What about the crimes committed by people in the name of God/gods? Terrorism, fundamentalism, insurgency, extremism, fanaticism etc. are linked to the excessive working of the **"spirituality"** spheres in people. The "spirituality" sphere overpowers the **"intelligence"** and acts with the active assistance of **"animality (instincts)"** to actualize their spiritual cravings. How does it work? In such situations, the **push factor** will be as under—

In Fig. 8.3 one sees all **push factors** (animality, spirituality, morality/ethics and intelligence). But, animality and

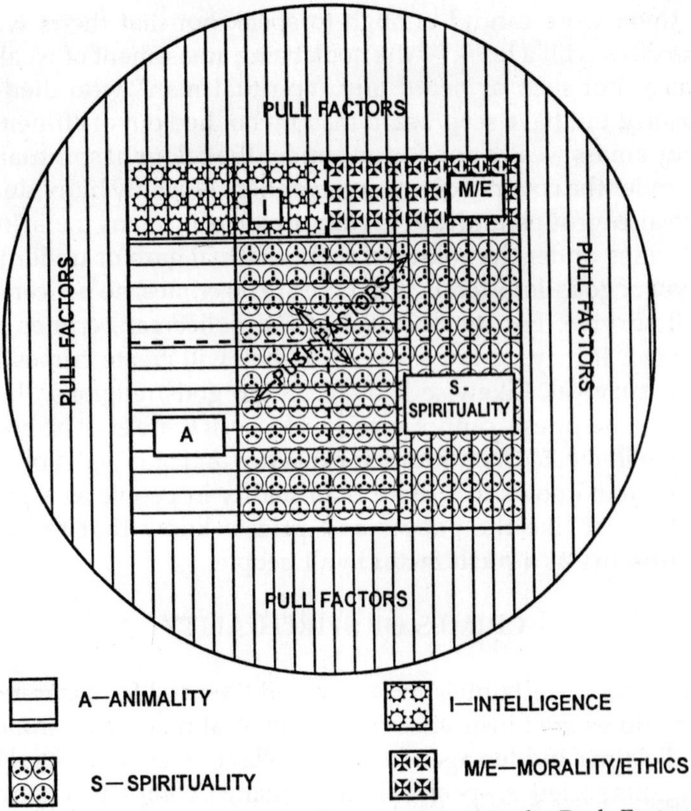

Fig. 8.3: Animality and Spirituality overpowering the Push Factors to form the Ego Factor (Animality and Spirituality work together to commit crimes).

spirituality work together to commit crimes. When they do the work, the other two factors—namely, **intelligence** and **morality/ethics** lie dormant or are almost devoured by **animality** and **spirituality.** In the Facebook, now I read :

> **"More people died owing to religion than of cancer, And, we are trying to find a cure for Cancer".**

Yes, there is a lot of truth in it. How many people are killed in the name of God/gods. In the Old Testament, Abraham was asked by God to sacrifice his only son for the pleasure of God and from thence, we see people being killed for God/gods or on behalf of God/god and for the greater glory/pleasure of God/gods. When I write this, I am seeing the religious terrorists killing people mercilessly and a *pujari* in north India was arrested for sacrificing a male child for the pleasure of God. How much property is burnt, destroyed and damaged by those who are religious terrorists? Even the culture, cultural institutions, monuments are burnt and destroyed. While it is done by the fundamentalists and fanatics, the spiritual men and religious people will give exhortations and pulpit sermons to the people that the atrocities committed by the fundamentalists/fanatics/terrorists are not what their religious Scriptures say or what their Almighty wants. While saying so, those who utter thus encourage, promote, incite and propel their religious adherents to continue their atrocities to the cruelest level possible. This is a game played by the religious top-ups who are criminals always and every time.

Just like any institutions doing business and trade, the religion and 'religious' men involve in trade and business in their own way. All malpractices, crooked ways of behaviour, illegalities and evil things in a business and trade are seen conducted by the religious groups. The hospital business and mission hospitals, educational institutions and charity centres, humanitarian works and man oriented services, orphanages and old age homes etc. are found to have business interests and many such institutions conducted by god-men and religious groups have become centres of crimes and illegalities. Why? There are films showing such illegal activities by religious men. Some of the *Asramas* are the breeding centres and later they promote illegalities including drug trafficking and other nefarious activities.

There is a saying in Malayalam : "Those who are close to a temple, mosque or church will be far away from God." Here, the concept of "God" is identified with "Goodness" and the saying reveals that those who are close to a temple, mosque or church will be far away from "Goodness". Exhibiting goodness, they involve in committing crimes of all kinds and every nature. Why? They can do them, because every man has **"spirituality"** in him as a **push factor** and so long as it is there, crimes can be sold without any difficulty—or with easiness.

People have **fear** as an emotion accompanying the instinct **escape.** Hence, many exploit this weakness and the advertisement industry survives on this particularly when they make advertisements on cosmetics, medicines, foodstuffs, baby food, tooth pastes, treatment modalities, body building equipments etc. They cheat the people and some times they offer incredible benefits by money chains, multi-marketing, investment frauds, resort *mafia,* escape from god's anger etc. How does it work?

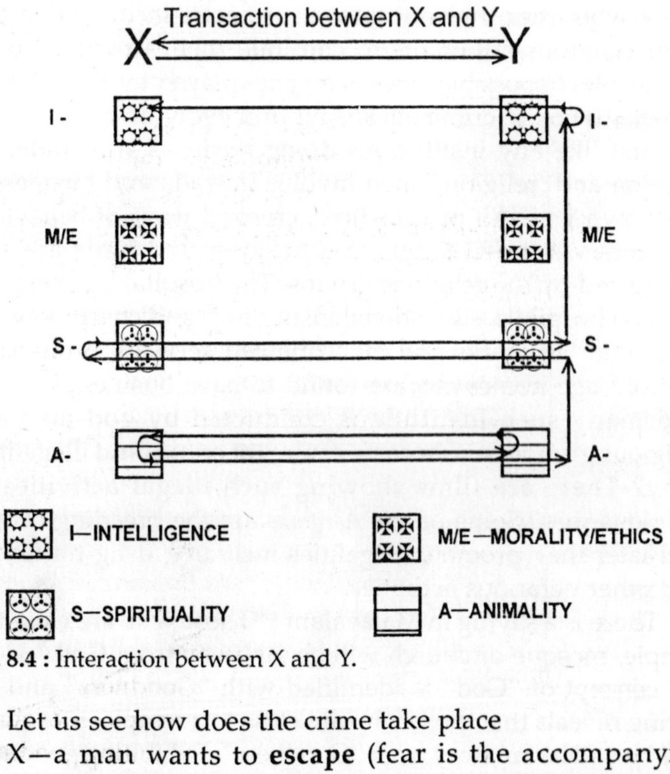

Fig. 8.4 : Interaction between X and Y.

Let us see how does the crime take place

X—a man wants to **escape** (fear is the accompanying emotion) from his anxiety. He wants to go to ***heaven*** and not to hell after death.

The religious, spiritual, god-man knows this. He is aware of the working of the instinct called **escape.** This **push factors**—escape goes from his **animality sphere.** The **push factor** falls on the **push sphere** of the god man 1, i.e., Y. He interacts from his **animality area** by returning **escape** (fear) as the **push factor.** As a result, he is distrubed, uncertainty is more, has hope. Again, he sends his **push factor** from the **animality sphere.**

The god man-Y, transfers the **push factor** to his **spirituality sphere** and gives hope and assurance. X feels happy and gets an assurance and informs Y that he is prepared to do anything if ***heaven*** is guaranteed to him. Y interacts from his **intelligence sphere** and convinces him to deposit Rs. 25000/- to get spiritual services after death. He does accordingly and becomes rich. The medical men, chartered accountants, businessmen, corporates, *Mafia* etc. involve in many such activities to amass wealth by illegal activities through interactions from the **spiritual sphere**. This is nothing, but cheating.

INTELLIGENCE AND CRIME

How does **intelligence** overpower other **push factors (animality, morality/ethics** and **spirituality)**? to form the **ego factor.** This is pictorially shown in the next page.

In Fig. 8.4, **intelligence** plays and can play an important role in the commission of crimes. As seen in (1), if Intelligence works with **animality** then any instinctual crimes can be committed with planning, design and well defined execution by individuals, institutions, groups and society. Murder is committed with calculated plans and execution strategies. In political murders, assassinations, murder for gain etc. one may see the role of intelligence working with **animality** as shown in Fig. 8.5 in the next page.

Activation Force

1. **Animality + Intelligence**
2. **Animality + Intelligence + Morality/Ethics**
3. **Animality + Intelligence + Spirituality**

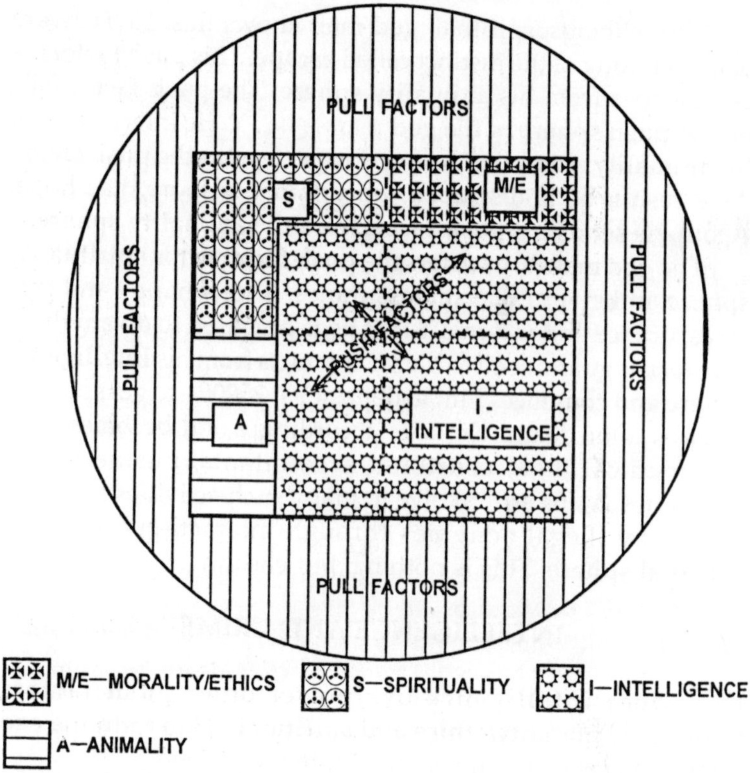

Fig. 8.5 : Intelligence overpowering the Push Factors to form the Ego Factor.

In Fig. 8.6, we may notice of all **push factors.** Nevertheless, animality and intelligence work together to commit the crimes. When they do the work, the other two **push factors,** *viz.,* **morality/ethics and spirituality** lie almost dormant or are devoured by **animality and intelligence.**

Earlier, scientists thought that the criminals were not intelligent. Their arguments were proved to be totally false by later researchers and it was categorically stated that the criminals were as intelligent as any other people and in some cases, more intelligent than most of the people. The I.Q. of the cyber criminals, Nexus criminals, international syndicate criminals and so on are found to be higher than many people

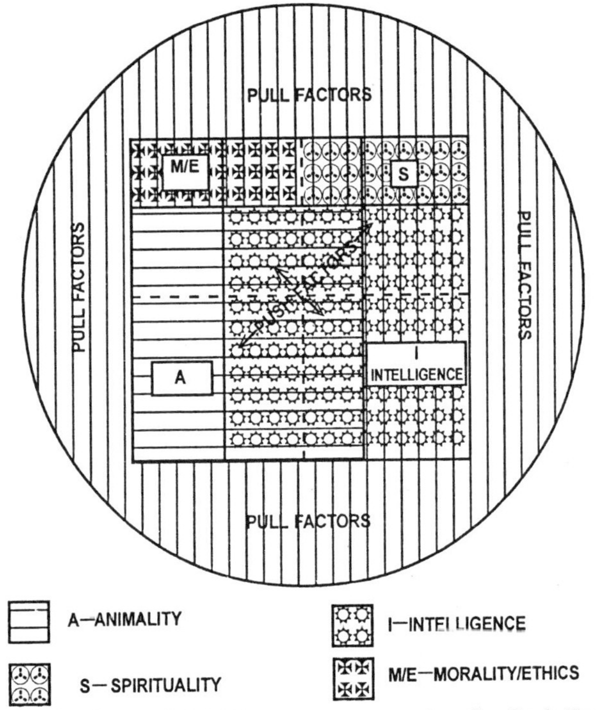

Fig. 8.6: Animality and Intelligence overpowering the Push Factors to form the Ego Factor (Animality and Intelligence work together to commit crimes).

in the world. I have seen police officials catching a thief to fetch a thief. For, the technology employed by some intelligent thieves is found to be very much superior even for very intelligent police investigators to understand it. What about those who hyjack air-planes?—Who work as spies?—Who involve themselves in bureaucratic crimes?—Who manage smuggling etc.

There are intelligent groups fully involved in planning and executing terrorist activities, killing people and actively participating in insurgency operations. Criminal gangs operating drug business, human traflicking, internet crimes, economic offences need high level I.Q. There are lawyer criminals who argue criminal cases logically and intelligently and they get acquittal verdicts from very intelligent judges.

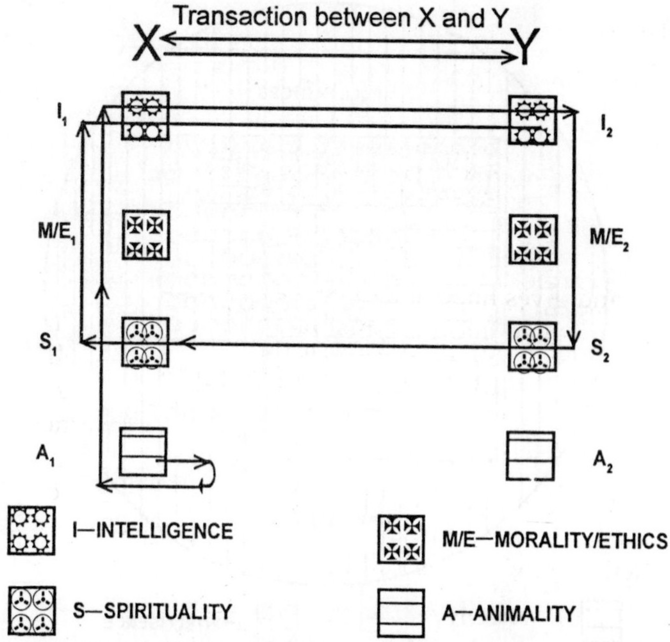

Fig. 8.7: Interaction between X and Y in a Victimological Crime.

There are countries which involve in the commission of intelligent crimes with an aim to destabilize the economic structure of another country. It has been noticed that some neighbouring countries which are hostile to India print and circulate Indian paper money to create a parallel economy. They are alleged to send trained terrorists to India. There are political parties which intelligently manage and manipulate matters to overthrow a Government in power and they do it by encouraging their political adherents to commit all sorts of crimes to create fear among the people.

X—a man/group wants to commit a crime, say-investment fraud. He/they offers/offer incredible rate of interest to the depositors—say, the principal amount will be multiplied to double within 30 months. Fine. Now, the crime—**investment fraud** starts from A_1—i.e., the **animal layer** but is sent from the I_1—**intellectual layer** to Y. It goes from X's **intellectual** I_1 layer to Y's **intellectual I_2 layer.** Y has anxiety about his future. His uncertainty in life creates a lot of frustrations, worries and mental conflicts. Here, he gets a **hope**—He believes in what X says. Because of X's belief and hope, he shows an inclination to X's proposal. X reacts from his S_1 layer and the interaction goes from S_1 to I_2 and finally the interation goes to X's I_1 and then accepted by Y's I_2. Here, Y becomes X's victim in a crime.

Thus, we see visa/N.O.C. rackets, investment *Mafia,* false employment bureaus, money chain and multi-marketing, relics sale and sale of *Elas* or *Bhasma* (in India), retreat treatments, prayer therapy, corruption of various types, bureaucratic crimes and what not? This is an example of **animality + intelligence + spirituality.**

Another example is from **animality + intelligence + morality/ethics.** As I said elsewhere, every crime has its "start" in **animality,** i.e., an instinct which is the activating force.

X—a man/group wants to commit a crime, say—a political strike or a labour strike. X wants to initiate a strike—i.e., an organized defiance to authority and he speaks of the moral

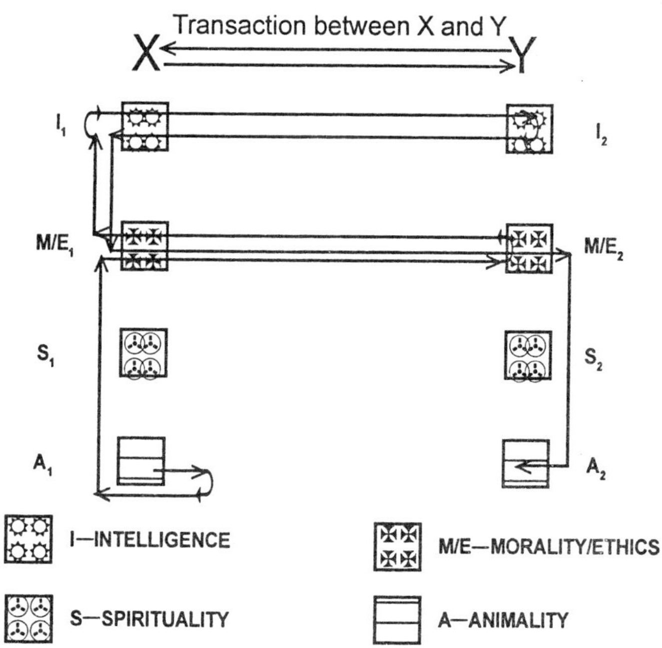

Fig. 8.8: Interaction for a Public Order Crime.

injustice to his followers. For this, he initiates his action from his A_1 and transfers it to the M/E_1. At that Y interacts from his M/E_2 and thus the interactions go on and X transfers them to I_1. From I_1, the movement is to I_2 of Y and from there to I_1 and from there to M/E_1 and from there to M/E_2 and from there to A_2 and thus one sees destruction of public property, damage to many things, law and order violations etc. I have studied this issue and I find that the animal ego activates the moral layer and thus the public order crimes take place throughout the world. Women's issues, labour strikes, students' agitations, agrarian unrest etc. are explained in this way.

Another real incident I have studied is as under. Here, the crime-doer was instigated by his wife to retaliate to an act committed by their neighbour in an Indian village. A dog belonging to the crime-doer went to the neighbouring house. It ate the food prepared there. The house wife saw the dog eating the food. She took a knife and threw at it. It was a mortal throw and the dog died after it reached its original home.

When the husband came home in the evening, his wife told everything about the dog and what happend in the neighbour's house. She attacked the moral sense to the extent of saying that the injury caused by the throw of the knife was as bad as stabbing her. To cut short, he took a butcher's knife and went to the neighbour's house. He had a quarrel and it was a heated quarrel with a lot of abusive words, hurting terms and filthy language. When the quarrel reached its peak, he took the butcher's knife and the lady of the house was brutally killed. The interaction was as shown in Fig. 8.9.

In Fig. 8.9, the interaction was from A_1 of X via M/E_1 to M/E_2 and back and from there to I_2 to I_1 and from there to A_1 of X resulting in the brutal murder of Y, the house wife of the neighbouring family.

In short, it can be said that every crime has a start at the **animal layer** and it ends with the instincts in the animal layer when crimes against human body is concerned. All Penal Codes have many sections of law showing the mental state, intention, motive etc. when they particularly define crimes against human body.

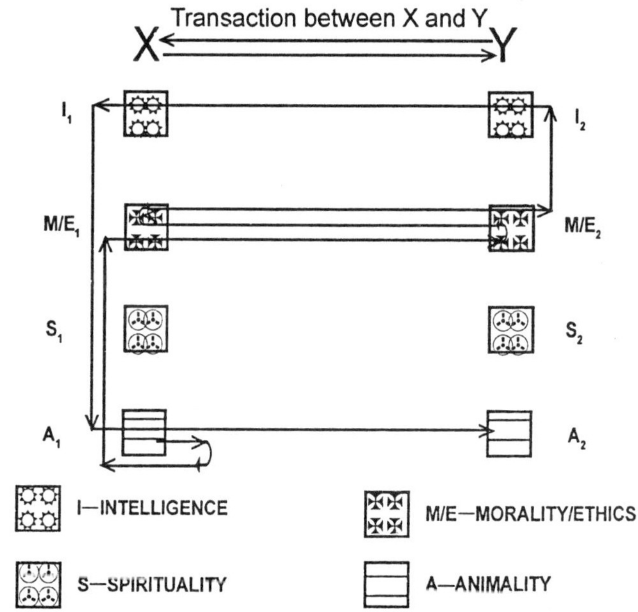

Fig. 8.9: Interaction for a Brutal Murder.

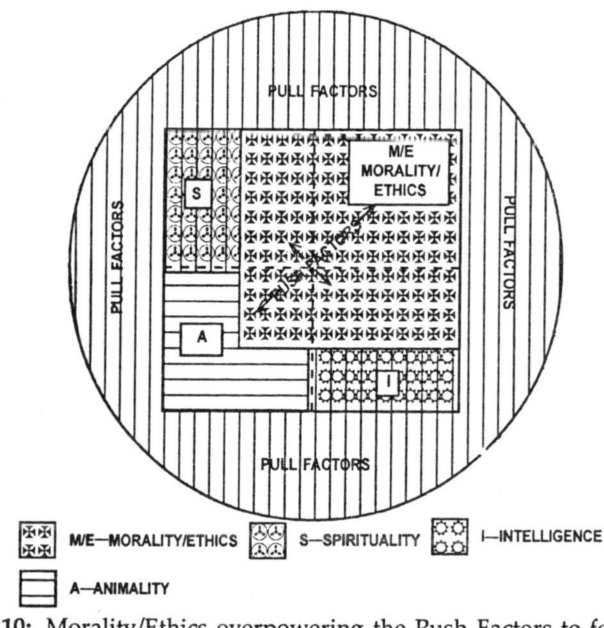

Fig. 8.10: Morality/Ethics overpowering the Push Factors to form the Ego Factor.

ETHICS AND MORALITY OVERPOWERING

How do **animality** and **intelligence** interact when crimes are committed? There are situations, intelligence does not work and in such cases, people call them "crimes of passion". In other words, they are crimes of animal instincts alone. There are crimes in which both instincts and intelligence work together.

In Fig. 8.11, the interactions go from A_1 to A_2 and backwards. The other layers—namely S, M and I are dormant or not interfering. The overpowering effect of the **animality layer** puts every other layers inactive or inoperative. This is what happens in murder, causing voluntary hurt or grievous hurt on sudden provocation etc. The intelligence, morality/ ethics or spirituality layers do not come so much so that there take place heated exchange of words, actions, signals, non-

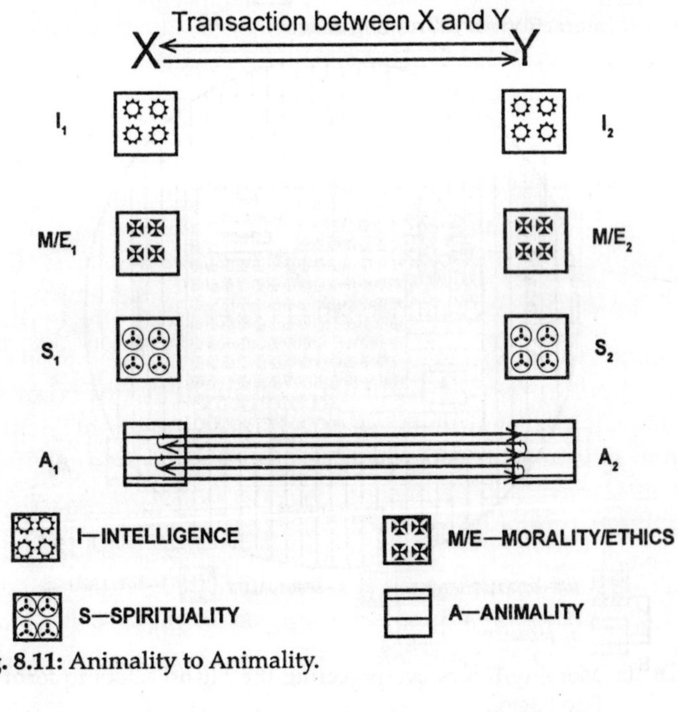

Fig. 8.11: Animality to Animality.

verbal behaviour etc. culminating in the physical attack, murder, sexual assault or affray of the other party.

ANIMALITY + INTELLIGENCE

This is as under—

In Fig. 8.12, it is seen that **animality** was expressed in a very intelligent manner. Everything is planned and executed. The means and methods are well designed earlier and as such we may say that the crime is well calculated and executed. In such cases, it may be difficult or very difficult to get evidence There may not be any eye-witnesses to prove the crime. There is the need to have scientific evidence. There is a case in which a lady injected tetanus germs to her friend and killed her. She had studied microbiology at the university level and made use of her knowledge and know-how to kill her friend in an intelligent way.

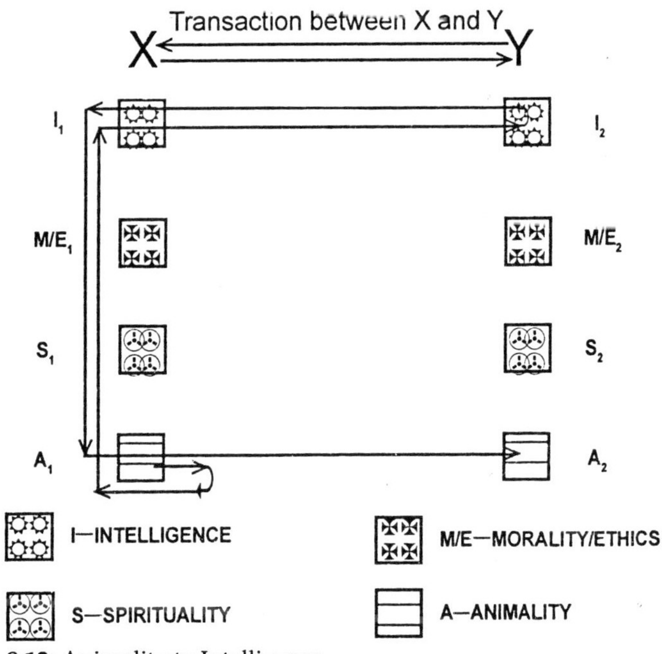

Fig. 8.12: Animality to Intelligence.

INTERACTION OF PUSH-PULL FORCES AND EGO FACTOR

Earlier, it was stated that the foundation of the **ego** and **ego factor** is laid by the time a child reaches its puberty. There takes place only the superstructure.

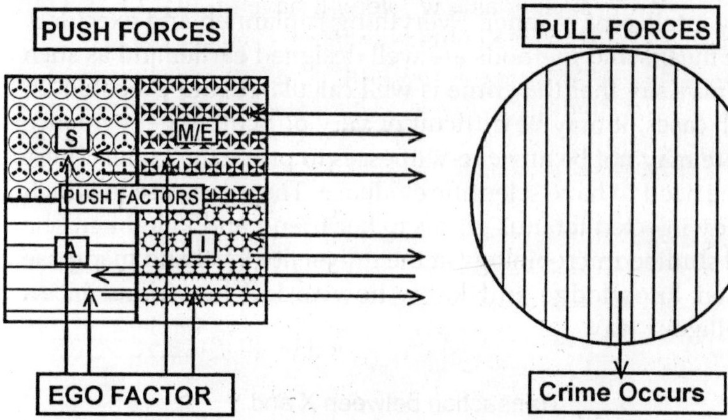

Fig. 8.13: Interaction of Push-Pull Forces and Ego Factor.

HOW? In a nutshell, the theory is as follows—

(1) Man is born with a heredity which interacts with the environment and forms the personality or ego.

(2) Man has four activating forces—**EGOS**—in his mind known as **animality, spirituality, morality/ethics** and **intelligence.** They are mixed together in such a way that the human mind works as one—the four energies in the **ego** are put under **push factors.**

(3) There are very many—*innumerable numbers—seen and unseen—heard and unheard—known and unknown—* environmental forces and situational factors around a man and all of them are put together to call them **PULL FACTORS.**

(4) Excuse me that I have to repeat what I said in the begining and thereafter repeatedly, i.e., from the birth of a child, the **PUSH** and **PULL FACTORS** interact to

form an **Ego** and **EGO FACTOR.** It is seen that the **foundation** of the **EGO FACTOR** is laid down by the time a person reaches his puberty. As a man grows older and older, the superstructure is constructed on this **foundation** and thus the **EGO FACTOR** gets modified to that extent. Like an individual, a group and a society as a whole will have an **EGO FACTOR** formed in due course.

(5) Whenever a man—a group—a society—is exposed to situations in life, the **PUSH FACTORS (animality + morality/ethics + intelligence + spirituality)** either fight or cooperate with the situations which are the **PULL FACTORS** at the given time, i.e.,

$$\text{C.B.} = \left\{ \begin{array}{c} \text{PULL FACTORS divided by PUSH FACTORS} \\ \text{or} \\ \text{PULL FACTORS multiplied by PUSH FACTORS} \end{array} \right\}$$

In other words—

$$\frac{\text{PULL FACTORS}}{\text{PUSH FACTORS}} \div$$

or $$\text{PULL FACTORS} \times \text{PUSH FACTORS}$$

Where

C.B. is Criminal Behaviour

The theory says—

1. When interaction takes place between the **PUSH FACTORS** in the already formed **EGO** or **PERSONALITY** and the **PULL FACTORS** presently available, a crime is committed if and when the **PULL FORCES** overpower the **PUSH FORCES.** In other words, an atmosphere contaminated with criminality or saturated with crimes exists, then commission of crime is the only option as the **EGO FACTOR** in the **PERSONALITY** is weak and incapable to fight with the **PULL FORCES.**

2. When the interaction takes place between **PUSH FACTORS** in the already formed **EGO or PERSONALITY** and **PULL FACTORS,** a crime is committed if and when the **ANIMALITY** without the support of other **PUSH FORCES** overpowers the **PULL FORCES,** putting down the effects of other **PUSH FACTORS** like **MORALITY/ETHICS, SPIRITUALITY and INTELLIGENCE.**
3. When the interaction takes place between the **PUSH FORCES** in the already formed **EGO or PERSONALITY** and **PULL FACTORS,** a crime is committed in a well calculated and planned way if and when the **ANIMALITY** and **INTELLIGENCE** jointly work and overpower the **PULL FORCES** lessening down the effects of other **PUSH FACTORS** like **MORALITY/ETHICS** and **SPIRITUALITY.**
4. A crime is sometimes committed by **ANIMALITY** with the support of either **SPIRITUALITY** or **MORALITY/ ETHICS** (and in some cases both) as the case may be.
5. Whenever the criminal prone **PUSH FACTORS** interact with **PULL FACTORS** which are crime prone by cooperation, then crimes will be the inevitable net result of such interactions.
6. The same theory is applicable in the case of individuals, groups or society alike.

Crimes can only be controlled or reduced in number. They can never be prevented *in toto* or eliminated from the society. If a particular type of crime is reduced, then there will come up another type of a similar crime. Thus, crimes are altered and never destroyed just like the energy which is neither created nor destroyed. It is changed from one form to another. Crimes are constant in a given society and I advocate a **QUOTA THEORY** of crime and I adhere to such an approach. Hence, reduction of crimes is possible and never their eradication at any stage/level. Man is blessed or condemned to live in crimes and amidst criminals. For, every human act/omission is an act/ omission prohibitted by some law or another; permitted by some law or another.

CONTROL AND REDUCTION OF CRIME AND CRIMINAL BEHAVIOUR

My research studies show that there are ways the crimes and criminal behaviour can be controlled or reduced. They are—

(1) Make the **PUSH FORCES** inactive or inoperative. For, crimes and criminal behaviour thrive only if there exists conducive atmosphere.

(2) Strengthen the **MORALITY** Factor by means and methods which will help to develop an upright conscience in the right direction. For, such a conscience will experience guilt feelings when one commits a crime/criminal behaviour.

(3) Inculcate values to develop a personality having **belief, faith or both** so that one will have adequate mental strength to have effective control over his self and behaviour. For a **Cosmic Power, a Supernatural Being** (God/s), a Universal Force, An Eternal/Absolute Principal **(spirituality)** have great strength and power to control man and his worldly (criminal in nature) behaviours.

(4) Train a person to control his animal instincts so that he acquires adequate strength to put them down—never permitting them to cross the threshold (boundary) to enter the criminality sphere. For, self-control of the instincts is the best control to reduce crimes and criminal behaviour.

(5) Enlighten the intelligence with information concerning laws, jurisprudence, justice, crimes, criminal behaviours, sins, vices, immorality, anti-social behaviour, injustice etc. and the ways and methods to control and reduce crimes in society. Education—academic, moral, religious, ethical, cultural, social etc.— is necessary for the purpose.

For all these manifold activities to be meaningfully performed, it is necesary to have a system of control and management of crimes. The system will consist of the family, schools, higher education centres, law abiding community/ neighbourhood, religious institutions, police, media, judiciary, executives and legislature etc. and they mean the formation of the ego factor in an upright way in the right direction—intellectually, morally/ethically, spiritually or by the control of animality in man. At the same time, one may accept and appreciate the fact that crimes/criminal behaviour can never be prevented *in toto*.

ANNEXURE

The WHY of various kinds of crimes is explainedd below.

Note: (i) As said repeatedly earlier, the **Ego Factor** is formed by the time an individual reaches his puberty. It is this **Ego Factor** which interacts with the Push Factors in later life.

(ii) Whenever two individuals interact, the interactions are between the two **Ego Factors** in them in the given **Pull Factors.**

(iii) There will be the **Ego Factor** for a group or a society as a whole. When groups/society have interactions, the **Ego Factor** behaves exactly like them behaving between two inividuals.

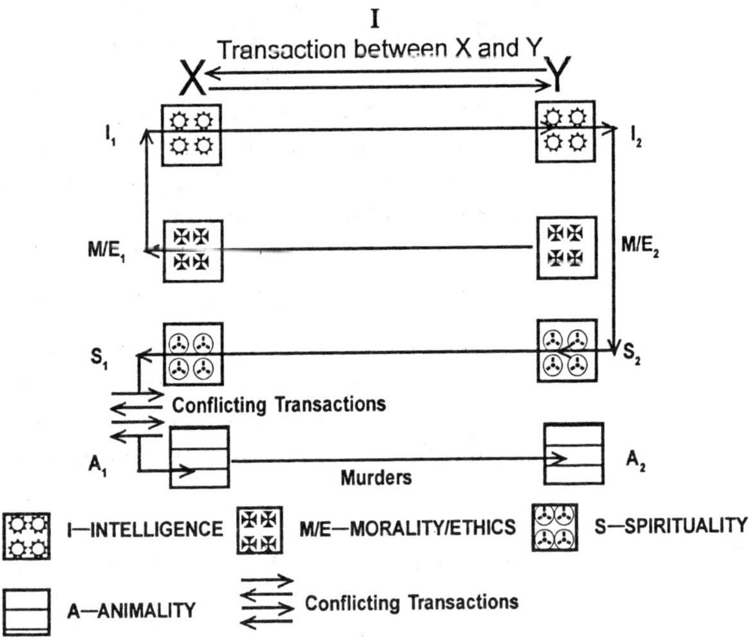

Fig. 8.14: Individual Crimes: Murder.

In Fig. 8.14—

(i) X and Y are **Lovers,** Y being the woman.

(ii) I_1 is **Intelligence Ego** of X and I_2 is the same of Y.
(iii) M/E_1 is **Morality/Ethics Ego** of X and M/E_2 is the same of Y.
(iv) S_1 is **Spirituality Ego** of X and S_2 is the same of Y.
(v) A_1 is the **Animality Ego** of X and A_2 is the same of Y.

The **Issue** in **Fact** : Murder of Y by X

Push Factors

(i) Dominant contents in the already formed **Ego Factor** in **Animality** are **Escape/and Pugnacity** with accompanying emotions of **Fear** an **Anger** respectively.
(ii) Dormant contents in the already formed **Ego Factor** are **Morality/Ethics, Spirituality** and **Intelligence.**

Pull Factors

Delay in marriage, pressure from the girl's family, rejection from the boy's family, conflicts, tensions, frustrations, social needs etc.

The **Facts in Issue :** X and Y are lovers for more than 5 years. X is 29 years old and Y is 28 years of age. Y does not want to delay her marriage. Here, family pressures her while the family of X rejects their affair. There is tension in both of them. Frustrations follow. One day, Y initiates her transactions from **M/E_2 Ego** and says : *"It is not morally correct to delay the marriage any longer."*

To this, X responds from his **I_1 Ego** and says : *"Yes, I know. But how can I maintain you without any income and family support"*. To this, Y answers : *"God will protect us and provide us the means and methods"* and thus, the transactions go on. Ultimately, X responds from his **A_1 Ego** and being activated from **Escape and Pugnacity,** he stabs her to death.

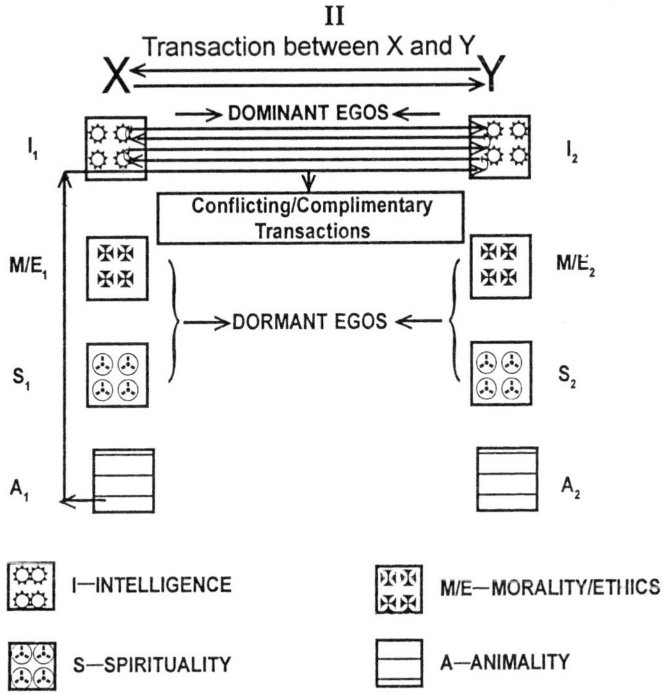

Fig. 8.15: Individual Crimes: White Collar Crimes

In Fig. 8.15—

(i) X, Y are two individuals.

(ii) I_1 & I_2 are the **Intelligence Egos** of X and Y respectively.

(iii) M/E_1 & M/E_2 are the **Morality/Ethics Egos** of X and Y respectively.

(iv) S_1 & S_2 are the **Spirituality Egos** of X and Y respectively.

(v) A_1 & A_2 are the **Animality Egos** of X and Y respectively.

The **Facts in issue**: X is the medical doctor and Y is his patient. She delivers an infant in his hospital. The doctor X being activated by **Acquisitiveness,** (with an emotion of feeling of ownership) initiates his transaction from his **I_1 Ego** and says that the baby needs to be in the incubator for a week as it has some breathing problems. She responds from her I_2 (by conflicting and complimentary transactions) and thus the baby is laid in the incubator paying Rs. 10,000/- per day.

Push Forces in the already formed **Ego Factor** is **Acquisitiveness,** in **Animality** while **M/E$_1$, M/E$_2$, S$_1$, S$_2$, A$_2$** etc. are dormant. The entire transactions take place between the **I$_1$** of **X** and the **I$_2$** of **Y**. It is a white collar crime as it is an anti-social act committed by a person of high socio-economic status to make money during the course of his profession without his victim knowing about the crime he commits.

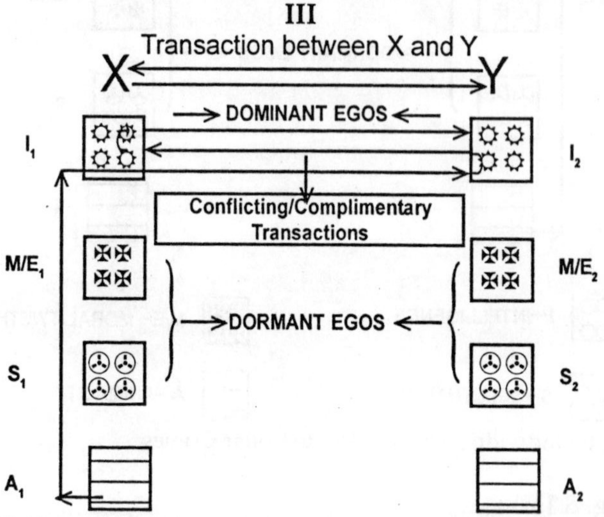

Fig. 8.16: Organized Crimes.

In Fig. 8.16—

(i) X and Y are individuals.
(ii) I$_1$ & I$_2$ are **Intelligence Egos**
(iii) M/E$_1$ & M/E$_2$ are **Morality/Ethics Egos**
(iv) S$_1$ & S$_2$ are the **Spirituality Egos**
(v) A$_1$ & A$_2$ are the **Animality Egos** of X and Y respectively.

The **Facts in issue** : X being a member in an organized syndicate, being activated from **Acquisitiveness (Animality)** to make exhorbitant profit by means, fair and foul, legal and illegal, engages in producing adulterated food products and sells them to people and lives as a malignant parasite which fattens on human weakness. His transactions are from the **Intelligence Ego** (I_1) to the **Intelligence Ego** (I_2) of Y and thus the crime is committed. The **M/E$_1$ & M/E$_2$, S$_1$ & S$_2$** of X and Y are dormant in the already formed **Ego Factor**. If they would have been active, the organized crime would not take place. Hence, in order to reduce the organized crimes in society, the **M/E** and **S Egos** must be activated in the already formed **Ego Factor** which interacts with the existing or available **Push Forces.**

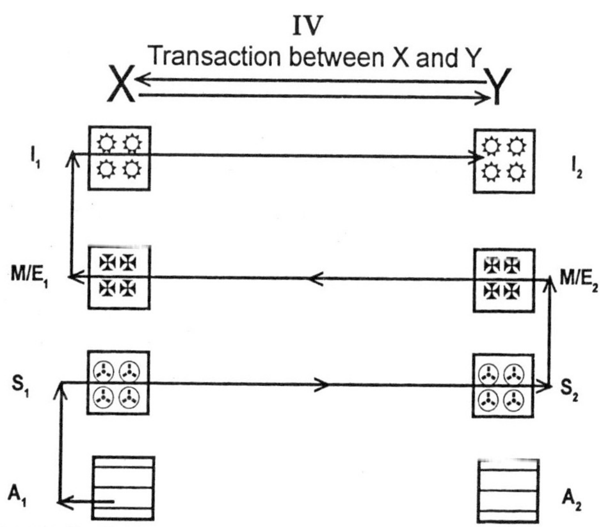

Fig. 8.17: Mafia Crimes.

In Fig. 8.17—

(i) X, Y—individuals.
(ii) I_1, I_2—**Intelligence Egos** of X and Y respectively.
(iii) M/E$_1$, M/E$_2$—**Morality/Ethics Egos** of X, Y respectively.
(iv) S_1, S_2—**Spirituality Egos** of X, Y respectively.
(v) A_1, A_2—**Animality Egos** of X, Y respectively.

Mafia (in U.S.A.) is a secret organization of persons, primarily assumed to be of Sicilian and mainland Italian origin engaged in criminal activities and in Sicily, it means a popular spirit of hostility to legal restraint and to the law, often manifesting itself in criminal acts (Webster's). *Mafia* had an origin in the thirteenth century in Italy and later in other European countries. The *Mafia* sale of the relics of Patre Pio in the west is notorious. Today, *Mafia* is used to mean all sorts of racketeering in local, regional, State, national or international levels. Thus, we have many types of *Mafia* and the aim is to make easy money in an illegal way. The already formed **Ego Factor** will have the dominance of animal instincts and they interact with the **Pull Factors**—i.e., facilitating environments to actualize the goals of the racketeering/*Mafia.* Depending upon the nature of the *Mafia,* the **Animality Ego** will travel through **Morality/Ethics Ego** [Charity *Mafia,* human service *Mafia* etc. are examples in point]. **Spirituality Ego** (Religious *Mafia,* Pilgrim *Mafia,* Disease-Cure *Mafia* etc. are examples in point) or **Intelligence Ego** (Educational *Mafia,* Examination *Mafia,* Expertise *Mafia* etc. are examples in point). In the interactions, the Dominant **Ego (Animality)** will play the vital part and other **Egos** will assist the dominant **Ego** to play its role in an effective way to commit crimes.

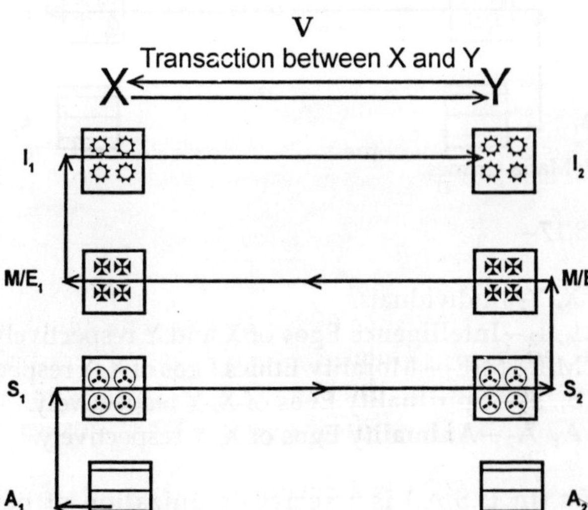

Fig. 8.18: Nexus Crimes.

In Fig. 8.18—

(i) X, Y are persons involved in nexus crimes.
(ii) I_1, I_2-M/E_1, M/E_2-S_1, S_2-A_1, A_2 are **Intelligence, Morality/Ethics, Spirituality** and **Animality Egos** in X, Y respectively.

Nexus crime has the characteristics of white collar crimes, organized crimes etc. with an unholy nexus among the Leaders, Bureaucrats, Businessmen, *gundas* and so on—i.e., *Neta* + *Babu* + *Dalal* + *Dada* in Indian culture. The *Dalal* is a middleman who plays an important role among the nexus partners. There is a ***nucleus*** and he may be a businessman around whom the *Neta,* Bureaucrats, *Dalal* and *Dadas* are singing and dancing to make money by nefarious means and methods by creating a linkage which is called an unholy nexus. Here too, the already formed **Ego Factor** will have the dominance of **Animality Egos** being assisted by **Morality/Ethics Egos** and **Spirituality Egos** to make exhorbitant profits by undesirable activities which are criminal in nature.

An overeffect of the **Morality/Ethics Egos** or **Spirituality Egos** may or can reduce the extent or intensity of the Nexus Crimes committed in the present-day society.

VI

JEL Crimes are a newcomers in criminology and they mean various crimes committed by the Judiciary, Executive and Legislature after making an unholy nexus/understanding among them. The Legislature makes the law, the Executive enforces the law and the Judiciary accepts/approves the law although they know that the law is illegal, immoral and unnderstandable or unintelligible. Here too, the **Animality** is the activating force and the **Spirituality, Morality/Ethics** and **Intelligence** accept, approve and assist the **Animality** to commit crimes.

In Fig. 8.19— X, Y are individuals **I_1, M/E_1, S_1, A_1** are the **Intelligence, Morality/Ethics, Spirituality** and **Animality Egos** of **X, I_2, M/E_2, S_2** and **A_2** are the same of **Y.**

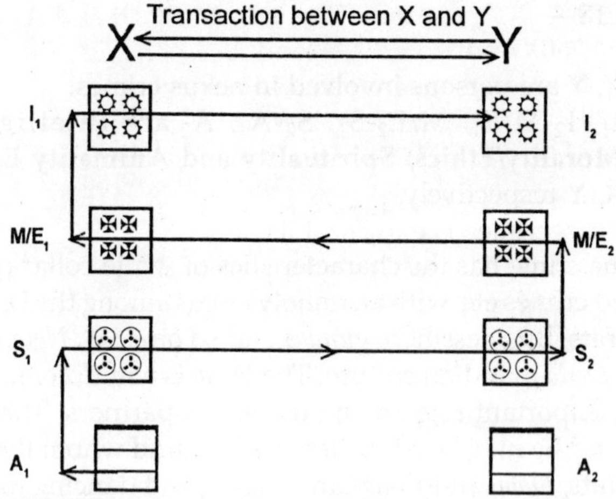

Fig. 8.19: *JEL* Crimes.

Now, many academicians and researchers speak about the museum piece nature of many laws enacted during eighteenth, nineteenth and twentieth century. They are used and misused to commit crimes and the Legislature is blind about them, Executive is silent about them. There exists a conspiracy of understanding and crimes are committed continuously for the advantage of vested interests.

VII

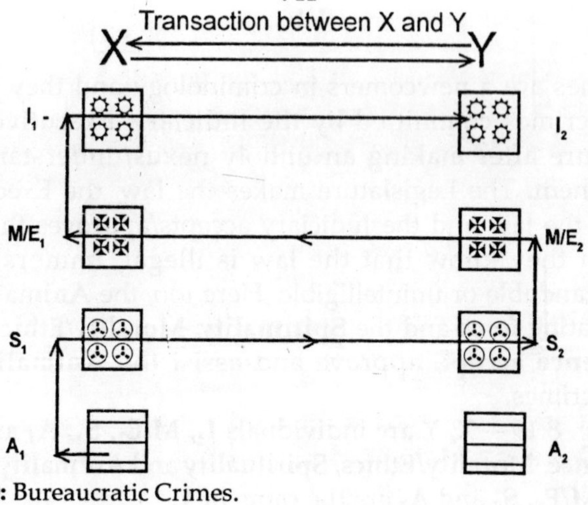

Fig. 8.20: Bureaucratic Crimes.

In Fig. 8.20 — X, Y are individuals $\mathbf{I_1}$, **M/E**$\mathbf{_1}$, $\mathbf{S_1}$ and $\mathbf{A_1}$ are the **Ego States** of **X** and $\mathbf{I_2}$, **M/E**$\mathbf{_2}$, $\mathbf{S_2}$ and $\mathbf{A_2}$ are the **Ego States** of **Y.**

Bureaucratic crimes are plenty and they are not seen in any Penal Codes. Hoarding of files, taking unjust decisions, accepting bribe, graft, illegal gratification, corruption, malpractices, concoction, false testimony, writing untruth and the litany of bureaucratic crimes is endless. Like any other crimes, the **Ego Factor** will have **Animality** as the projected **Ego** with instincts (accompanying emotions) to achieve the goal. Here too, the **Animality Ego** is supported, assisted or assured of by **Morality/ Ethics Ego** and **Spirituality Ego** which are relatively not very fiercely in operation. The ultimate objective of the commission of bureaucratic crimes will be to the benefits of the bureaucrats. Bureaucratic crimes may have nexus partners and some times the elements of white collar crimes may be seen. Proper vigilance and supervision may effect a control over the bureaucratic crimes, nevertheless, an excessiveness of the **animal insitncts** will make the bureaucrats to involve in the commission of very many crimes for lucrative advantage and pecuniary benefits.

VIII

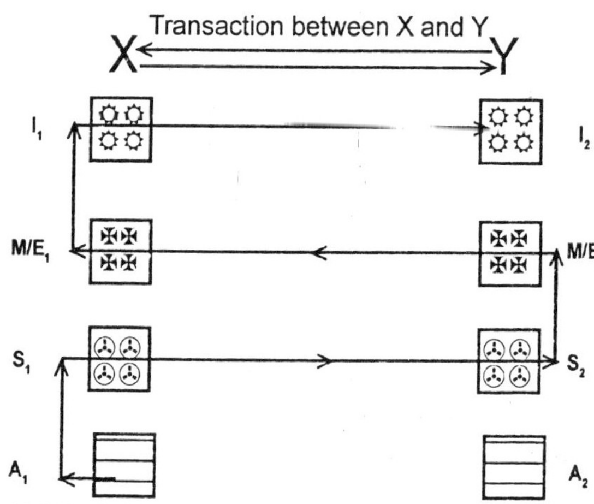

Fig. 8.21 : Political Crimes.

In Fig. 8.21—X, Y are individuals $\mathbf{I_1}$, $\mathbf{I_2}$, **M/E**$\mathbf{_1}$, **M/E**$\mathbf{_2}$, $\mathbf{S_1}$, $\mathbf{S_2}$, $\mathbf{A_1}$, $\mathbf{A_2}$ are the **Egos** of **Intelligence, Morality/Ethics, Spirituality** and **Animality** of X and Y.

Political crimes are not defined in the Penal Codes as they are new-comers. The concept of political crimes is different from the concept of traditional crimes. The aim of the political offender is to change the political system or a Government policy, protest national security, react to public order etc. No doubt, the **Animality** (with instincts and accompanying emotions) is supported by **Intelligence Ego** for its planning and execution. The political criminal may have moral/ethical justification for what he does and precisely therefore, the political crime is assisted by the **Morality/Ethics Ego**. There may be, pure political crimes and *'complex'* or *'connected'* offences. Treason, sedition, espionage, other acts of endangering the external security of the State, rebellion, incitement to civil war etc. are all considered pure political crimes. Here, **Animality + Intelligence + Morality/ Ethics Egos** will jointly work for the success. Offences that endanger the life and property of people but are carried out in connection with and in furtherance of various crimes against the State/Souvereign might be shown as *connected or complex* to political offences. Here, the **Animality** is the most **dominant Ego** and others, of course, are powerful indeed.

IX

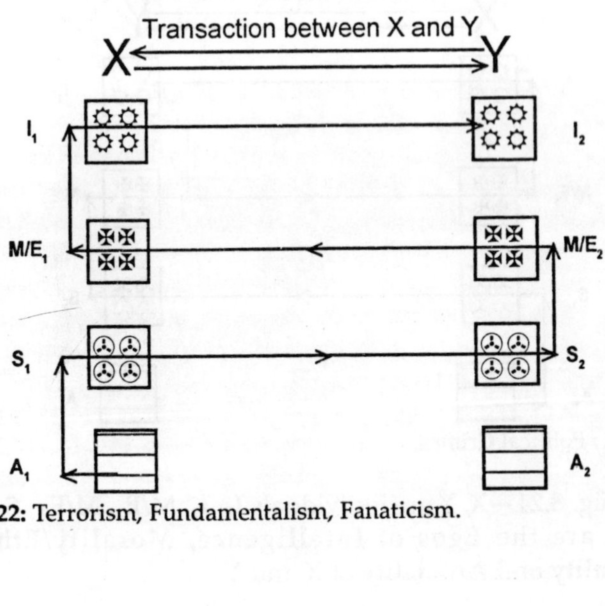

Fig. 8.22: Terrorism, Fundamentalism, Fanaticism.

In Fig. 8.22—X, Y are individuals I_1, M/E_1, S_1 and A_1 are the **Intelligence Ego, Morality/Ethics Ego, Spirituality Ego** and **Animality Ego** in **X** and I_2, M/E_2, S_2 and A_2 are the same of **Y.**

Terrorism is closely connected to causing intense, sharp and overmastering fear. A terrorist may be motivated by political considerations (**Intelligence Ego**). A fundamentalist may be motivated by religious considerations (**Spirituality Ego**) and a fanatic may be a person with extreme and uncritical enthusiasm or zeal, as in religion (**Spirituality Ego**), politics (**Intelligence Ego**) etc. and in all such cases, the activating energy can be from the **Animality Ego**—namely, **Escape** (emotion is **Fear**), **Repulsion** (emotion is **Disgust**), **Pugnacity** (emotion is **Anger**) etc. In all such criminal activities, the strategy of action usually is to attack the masses—to attack the people in such a way that it is the Government/religion which appears to be their enemy. All of them have their commitment to violence (**Pugnacity**). The **Ego Factor** as stated everywhere and elsewhere is the product of the interactions between the **Push** and **Pull Factors.** (Fig. 8.23)

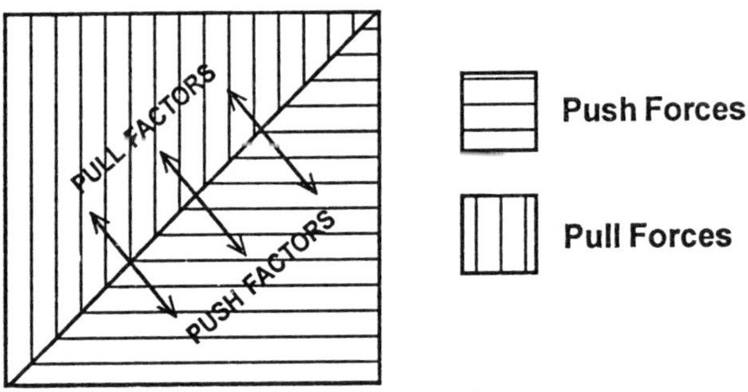

Fig. 8.23: Interaction between Push and Pull Factors.

As a result of the interactions between the **Push** and **Pull Factors,** an **Ego Factor** is formed. The foundation of this **Ego Factor,** as repeatedly said earlier, is laid down by the time a person reaches his/her puberty. The **Ego Factor** then will be as as shown in Fig. 8.24.

The **Intelligence, Spirituality** and **Morality/Ethics Egos** control or regulate the **Animality**—energy given by animal

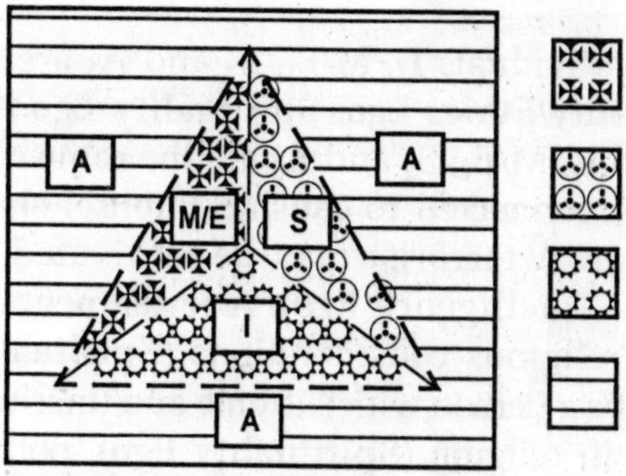

Fig. 8.24: Formation of the Ego Factor.

instincts. The **Ego Factor** already formed in an individual interacts with the **Pull Factors** in later life. During the interaction, one of the **Egos** in the **Ego Factor** will dominate and they can be drawn as shown in Fig. 8.25.

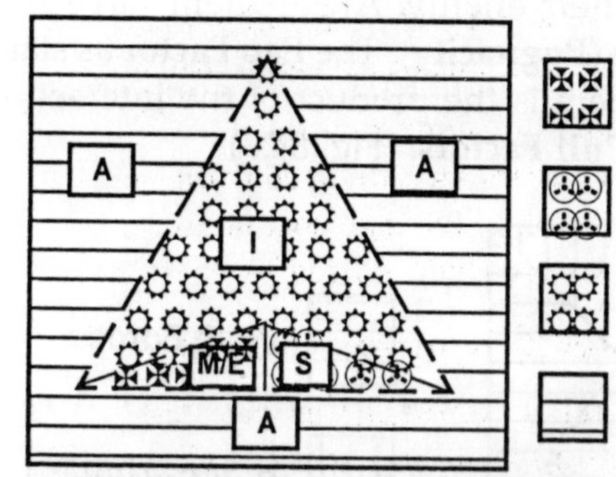

Fig. 8.25 (a): Domination of Intelligence Ego.

Illustrations

1. In terrorism, fundamentalism, fanaticism, **Spirituality** may dominate. If it is not uprightly formed in the right direction, crimes may be resulted. No crime will be committed if the **Spirituality** is uprightly formed in the right direction.
2. In terrorism, fundamentalism, fanaticism etc., **Morality/Ethics** may dominate. If it is not uprightly

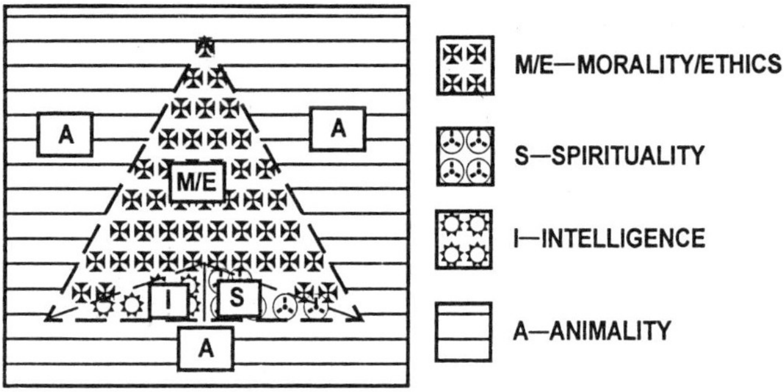

Fig. 8.25 (b): Domination of Morality/Ethics Ego.

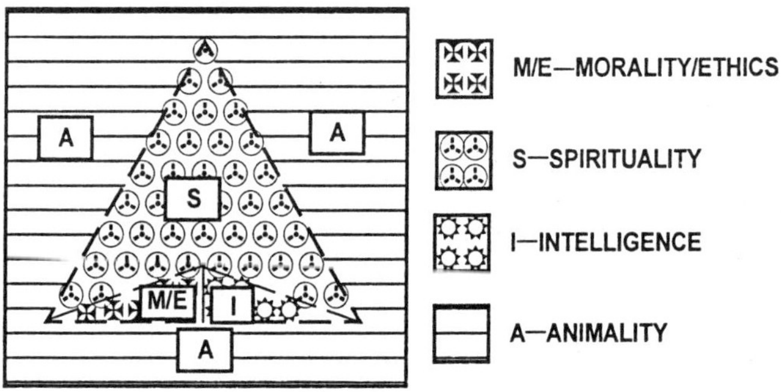

Fig. 8.25 (c): Domination of Spirituality Ego.

formed in the right direction, crimes will be resulted in various forms.

3. In terrorism, fundamentalism, fanaticism etc., **Intelligence** may dominate. If it is not uprightly formed in the right direction, crimes will be resulted in different ways.

It may be remembered that the **Pull Factors** play an important role in the formation of the **Intelligence, Morality/ Ethics** and **Spirituality Egos** uprightly in the right direction.

Special Note

The explanation given above in the commission of various types of individual crimes will be applicable, *mutatis mutandis,* to group and society crimes as Group and Society have the Ego Factors just like the individuals have them.

Notes

1. Precipitating factors/causes mean those which hasten the occurrence of—bring about prematurely, hastily, or suddenly (Webster's).
2. Predisposing means to give an inclination or tendency to beforehand.

Bibliography

Authoritative and Authentic books authored by Dr. James Vadackumchery in the special areas of crime, police and justice.

Acquittals in Administration of Justice, (1983) Ph.D. Thesis, Kerala University, (mimeo), Thiruvananthapuram.

Activism, Accountability and Justice (2004) *(ISBN: 81-7341-4324-X)*, Indian Publishers' Distributors, New Delhi.

Bankers' Safety: Methods and Techniques, (2002) *(ISBN: 81-7022-937-5)*, (Second edition), Concept Publishing Company (P) Ltd., New Delhi.

Child Labour (Malayalam), (2000) State Literacy Mission, Thiruvananthapuram.

Contemporary Indian Criminology (2015), ***(ISBN : 978-93-5125-100-2)***, Concept Publishing Company (Pvt.) Ltd., New Delhi.

Crime and Society : Current Issues and Trends, (1999) ***(ISBN: 81-7648-024-X)***, A.P.H. Publishing Corporation, New Delhi.

Crime, Law and Police Science, (2003) *(ISBN: 81-7022-995-2)*, (Second edition), Concept Publishing Company (P) Ltd., New Delhi.

Crime, Police and Correction, (1998) *(ISBN: 81-7024-939-2)*, A.P.H. Publishing Corporation, New Delhi.

Criminology and Penology, (1983) Kairali Books International, Trivandrum.

Departmental Inquiries and Injustice, (1997) *(ISBN: 81-7024-899-X)*, A.P.H. Publishing Corporation, New Delhi.

Goodbye, Police: Memoirs of a Criminologist, (2005) *(ISBN: 81-7341-390-8)*, Indian Publishers' Distributors, New Delhi.

Human Behaviour and Law Enforcement, (1995) ***(ISBN: 81-7024-688-1),*** Ashish Publishing House, New Delhi.

Human Relations in Banking: How to get along better with people?, (1988) Santha Publishing House, Cochin.

Human Rights : A Fair Trial of United Nations (Vol. I) Concept Publishing Company (Pvt.) Ltd., New Delhi, (Under Publication).

Human Rights : A Fair Trial of United Nations (Vol. II) Concept Publishing Company (Pvt.) Ltd., New Delhi, (Under Publication).

Human Rights and the Police in India, (1996) ***(ISBN: 81-7024-722-5),*** A.P.H. Publishing Corporation, New Delhi.

Human Rights Friendly Police: A Myth or Reality?, (2000) ***(ISBN: 81-7648-150-5),*** A.P.H. Publishing Corporation, New Delhi.

Human Values and Police Behaviour, (2000), Bureau of Police Research and Development, Ministry of Home Affairs, Government of India.

India's Supreme Court and Police: Consensus and Conflicts, (2003) ***(ISBN: 81-7341-301-0),*** Indian Publishers' Distributors, New Delhi.

Indian Police 2001: What Went Wrong Here? (1998) ***(ISBN: 81-7024-967-8),*** A.P.H. Publishing Corporation, New Delhi.

Indian Police and Equal Justice Under Law, (1999) ***(ISBN: 81-7648-066-5),*** A.P.H. Publishing Corporation, New Delhi.

Indian Police and Miscarriage of Justice, (1997) ***(ISBN: 81-7024-792-6),*** A.P.H. Publishing Corporation, New Delhi.

Indian Police and Nexus Crime, (2002) ***(ISBN: 81-7835-037-8),*** Kalpaz Publications, Delhi.

Judiciary and Juvenile Justice, (2005) ***(ISBN: 81-7341-389-4),*** Indian Publishers' Distributors, New Delhi.

Juvenile Delinquency (2000) (Malayalam), State Literacy Mission, Thiruvananthapuram.

Kolayalikalude Pinnampuram, (Malayalam) (2015), ***(ISBN : 81-7705-321-0)*** Prabhath Book House, Thiruvananthapuram..

Kuttakrithyangalile Kazhukanmar, (Malayalam) (2014) ***(ISBN : 978-81-300-1598-9),*** Poorna Publications, Kozhikode.

Kuttakrithyangalude Baliyadukal, (Malayalam) Poorna Publications, Kozhikode [To be released soon].

Management Thoughts for Justice Administration, (2013), **[*ISBN : 13-978-81-7268-233-0* (HB)],** Logos Press, New Delhi.

Management Thoughts on Police Administration, (1998) ***(ISBN: 81-7024-914-7),*** A.P.H. Publishing Corporation, New Delhi.

Misguiding Philosophies and Millennium Police, (2003) ***(ISBN: 81-7341-278-2),*** Indian Publishers' Distributors, New Delhi.

National Police Commission: Issues for Rethinking, (1998) ***(ISBN: 81-7024-826-4),*** A.P.H. Publishing Corporation, New Delhi.

Police and Human Rights, (ed.), (1994) Kerala Police Officers' Association, Thiruvananthapuram.

Police and the People (2000), (Translation of the title: Public Relations at the Cutting Edge Level: Case-study materials by Prof. C.K. Muhammed Ummer), The State Institute of Language, Kerala, Thiruvananthapuram.

Police and the Society, (1985), Kairali Books International, Trivandrum.

Police Criminology and Crimes, (2002) *(ISBN: 81-7835-094-7),* Kalpaz Publications, Delhi.

Police Enforcement Crimes and Injustice, (2001) *(ISBN: 81-212-0471-5),* Gyan Books Ltd., New Delhi.

Police Interrogation: DOs which the Police do not DO, (1998) *(ISBN: 81-7024-974-0),* A.P.H. Publishing Corporation, New Delhi.

Police Leadership: The Inside Story, (1999) *(ISBN: 81-7648-120-3),* A.P.H. Publishing Corporation, New Delhi.

Police Morality, (2001) *(ISBN: 81-7835-038-6),* Kalpaz Publications, Delhi.

Police, Victim and Victim Justice, (2001) *(ISBN: 81-7479-043-8),* Kaveri Books, New Delhi.

Police, Women and Gender Justice, (2000) *(ISBN: 81-7648-137-8),* A.P.H. Publishing Corporation, New Delhi.

Policing the Largest Democracy: 50 Years and After, (1998) *(ISBN: 81-7024-979-1),* A.P.H. Publishing Corporation, New Delhi.

Policing the Police: A Nation's Cry, (2003) *(ISBN :81-7479-060-81),* Kaveri Books, New Delhi.

Professional Police Witness Interviewing, (1999) *(ISBN: 81-7648-061- 4),* A.P.H. Publishing Corporation, New Delhi.

Public Relations at the Cutting Edge Level: Case-study Materials, (1985), National, New Delhi.

Road Users' Guide (1997) (Malayalam), Assistant Motor Vehicle Inspectors' Association, Ernakulam.

Singapooril Ninnoru Kuttapathram, (Malayalam) Prabhath Book House, Thiruvananthapuram, [To be released soon].

Society, Police and Crimes: Tasks and Challenges, (2002) *(ISBN: 81-7341-266-0),* Indian Publishers' Distributors, New Delhi.

Sociology of Policing India: 2000 and Beyond, (2003) *(ISBN: 81-7341-279-0),* Indian Publishers' Distributors, New Delhi.

The Complete Reference Methodology of Research in Criminology Law, Justice and Correction (2007), **(Vol. I)**, *(ISBN: 81-7341-414-8),* Indian Publishers' Distributors, New Delhi.

The Complete Reference Methodology of Research in Criminology Law, Justice and Correction (2010) **(Vol. II)**, ***(ISBN: 81-7341-448-0),*** Indian Publishers' Distributors, New Delhi.

The Complete Reference Methodology of Research in Criminology Law, Justice and Correction (2010), **(Vol. III)**, ***(ISBN: 81-7341-449-7),*** Indian Publishers' Distributors, New Delhi.

The Justice Less Administered, (2005) ***(ISBN: 81-7341-380-0),*** Indian Publishers' Distributors, New Delhi.

The Police and Delinquency in India, (1996) ***(ISBN: 81-7024-725-X),*** A.P.H. Publishing Corporation, New Delhi.

The Police, The Accused and Criminal Injustice, (1997) ***(ISBN: 91-7024-806-X),*** A.P.H. Publishing Corporation, New Delhi.

The Police, the Court and Injustice, (1997) ***(ISBN: 81-7024-806-X),*** A.P.H. Publishing Corporation, New Delhi.

The Police, The People and Criminal Justice, (1999) ***(ISBN: 81-7024-862-9),*** A.P.H. Publishing Corporation, New Delhi.

The Unseen Phases of Crimes, *(Malayalam),* (2009) ***(ISBN: 81-909360-1-8),*** H&C Publishing House, Trissur.

Third Millennium Police: Take off Trends in India, (1999) ***(ISBN: 81-7648-062-2),*** A.P.H. Publishing Corporation, New Delhi.

U.N. Universal Declaration of Human Rights and Criminal Justice: The Total Revision (2012) **(*ISBN : 13-978-81-8069-912-2*)** Concept Publishing Company (Pvt.) Ltd., New Delhi.

United Nations and Indian Mysticism: Parallels on Human Rights and Police, (2002) ***(ISBN: 81-7022-664-2),*** Concept Publishing Company (P) Ltd., New Delhi.

United Nations and Prison Justice : The Complete Revision of the Standard Minimum Rules for the Treatment of Prisoners, (*ISBN : 978-818-069-9610*), Concept Publishing Company (Pvt.) Ltd., New Delhi, 2014.

Values and God's Commandments, (1995) (Malayalam) Catechetical Centre, Thalassery.

Why I am not a Policeman, (2001) ***(ISBN: 81-7479-042-X),*** Kaveri Books, New Delhi.

Wounded Justice and the Story of Indian Police, (2001) ***(ISBN: 81-7479-045-4),*** Kaveri Books, New Delhi.

Index